The Organized Startup

Setting things right from the start to prevent oversights

Emica Mao

Copyright © 2022 Emica Mao

All rights reserved.

ISBN: 9798461547295

DEDICATION

To startup founders –

Though learning from your own mistakes is good, you don't have to necessarily experience them in order to learn. You can learn from what others have gone through.

May this book help you navigate your startup journey smarter and help you prevent avoidable mistakes.

CONTENTS

	Preface	i
1	Are you Ready?	1
2	Setting up a Company	15
3	Accounting & Finance	41
4	HR	53
5	Legal & Corporate Compliance	61
6	Master Data Room	69
7	Employee Stock Options	77
8	Fund-Raising & Share-Related Matters	87
	Conclusion	109
	Annex	119
	Message from the Author	131

PREFACE

In the last 10 years I have worked with startup founders in Asia, I have noticed a common pattern - when the company starts its operations, founders primarily focus their energies on developing the product, gaining traction and generating revenues, while other functions stay only in the periphery. Then after a few months, little problems arise such as:

- The figures the founders have been presenting to prospective investors do not match the figures declared by the accountant in the financial statement. Apparently, they have never aligned on how to recognize revenues, and classify and accrue expenses.
- The company's corporate structure was not well-thought of and as a result, the original entity that was set up has to be dissolved and a new entity incorporated.
- Board resolutions were forgotten to be executed for some major company decisions and the board is not too happy with the founders' negligence.
- A couple of months after the accountant resigned, the founders realized that there are some records that were not turned over. Unfortunately, the accountant is no longer answering calls and messages.
- Founders have difficulty in recalling and explaining their cap table's history to prospective investors.
- For the lack of a proper online filing system in place, founders waste a lot of time searching through past email and chat threads every time

they need to trace company documents and agreements.
- The company has impending threats of labor complaints from disgruntled employees.

These are just some examples, among many potential issues, that could bog down founders in their startup journey. The worst consequences which I have seen were filed lawsuits, labor complaints, huge tax penalty fees - all resulting to loss of trust in the founders by shareholders and investors. Time spent on fixing such problems is time taken away from growing the business. And it is not easy to recover from situations like these – assuming one can recover from it at all.

A single oversight can potentially wipe out all of a founder's hard work. Thus, I wrote this book to help founders organize their startups - from the very start of their journey – so they could prevent avoidable mistakes that could cost a lot to fix, or worse, a single oversight that could cost everything a founder has worked so hard for.

With this book, may founders be spared from painful experiences which other startup founders have gone through. Though learning from one's own mistakes is good, one doesn't have to necessarily experience them in order to learn.

- Emica Mao

The Organized Startup

1 ARE YOU READY?

When you're starting a new company, it's bootstrap mode. Typically, it is just you and your co-founders splitting all the work across the different functions – sales & marketing, product development, operations, accounting & finance, and HR. Or if no one is familiar with a certain function, or no one has bandwidth to accommodate any more responsibilities, you might hire a staff or outsource the work to a consultant or third party to keep the headcount low.

You will find yourself working late hours and on weekends, but even then, there is never enough time to do everything. Given the time constraint, logic would dictate that you should focus on the most important things – the work that would bring you closer to achieving your company's target milestones in time for the next fund-raise - which typically revolve around product development, sales & marketing and operations. The other functions somehow become secondary priorities.

Along the way though, some things start falling through the cracks and you may find yourself in situations such as -

- The revenue figures in your KPI tracker do not match the figures declared by the accountant in the financial statements.
- Direct costs were not properly classified in the books. This means that the unit economics you have been presenting to prospective investors is not accurate.
- A consultant missed to receive his professional fee on time because no one shared the consultancy contract with the staff processing the payroll.
- You knew that cash runway is still good for 12 months, but after only a few months into the year, the cash runway got shorter to 6 months. What just happened?
- It's audit season and the auditor is asking for the supporting board resolution for a certain company transaction (which requires board approval as stated in the by-laws). Unfortunately, no one executed the required paperwork.
- The accountant resigned and though he turned over some files, it was only after a few months after he left when the company realized that there are some files not turned over. Sadly, the old accountant is no longer answering any of the company's calls and messages.

These are just some examples of potential situations which you might find yourself into, and though some may sound minor, when such oversights and mistakes are compounded over time, your company could be in a real mess. For example, if there are discrepancies in your financials, how do you know that your company is making real progress? If direct costs are not properly recognized, how certain are you that you are making a profit on every transaction?

If your startup has missing documents, incurred tax penalties and has received a number of labor-related complaints, what do you think would be the level of confidence and trust of prospective investors and your existing shareholders in you? It is definitely not a good sign if you cannot get things right and manage the business well while you're still small and just starting.

This snowball of oversights would eventually haunt and bog down startup founders. Putting off fires here and there is just a band-aid solution. The game plan of some founders is to just clean up the mess by hiring lawyers, accountants, and professionals at a later time (when the company is able to raise funds or when it starts generating significant revenues), but that is not exactly a good plan. Why?

First, it may cost more to hire professionals to fix mistakes and clean up the mess, rather than simply preventing them from happening in the first place.

Second, when you are raising funds, you won't look good to potential investors during the due diligence process since they may conclude that you do not take corporate governance matters seriously. Continued negligence would not also sit well with your existing shareholders and board and may lead to an eventual loss of integrity and trust.

Third, there may be mistakes that can only be fixed at a very high cost, or worse, mistakes that unfortunately cannot be fixed at all.

That is why it's important that just as you are starting your company, you should proactively lay an organized and clear foundation for your company, instead of reactively dealing with issues as they come along. The good news is - such oversights could be avoided - if only you start with proper frameworks right from the very beginning of your startup journey. And this is what the book is about. It is (1) to help you think about some important aspects of the business which are oftentimes overlooked, and (2) to help you learn how to develop and customize frameworks (based on the local requirements and regulations applicable to your company's domicile) which could serve as your guides in managing your startup.

Aspects of the business which are often overlooked or given less priority are typically those that require a lot of administrative work and documentation such as accounting, HR, legal, corporate governance and anything that is equity-related. Thus, this book focuses on organizing and establishing frameworks in these areas (and not about product development, operations and sales & marketing since a lot of other books have been written about these subjects already).

Frameworks presented in the book are domicile-agnostic as it is very challenging to customize the content to a specific country since regulations and requirements vary not just from country to country, but from one industry to another, and they are also unpredictably subject to change.

The frameworks and checklists presented here are also intended to serve as your starting point, then you can edit and build on them based on your company's nature of business and what is required and allowed in your place of operations. To customize your checklists, it is your duty to check the latest regulations and requirements in your company's domicile by consulting with a local lawyer or local expert.

The frameworks and checklists presented here would also help guide you into thinking about the right questions to ask your service providers (e.g. lawyers and accountants). Some major problems experienced by other startups arise from situations where the right questions were never asked by the founders. Unfortunately, when the right questions are not asked, some essential information may be inadvertently omitted, or some potential scenarios may not be scoped, considered or foreseen. Oftentimes, the omissions are not intentional. The service provider may simply have assumed that the startup founder already knew that is why he/she never asked.

As a general rule, to prevent this from happening, be transparent with your lawyer, accountant or service provider if a certain topic is something new to you and/or you have little knowledge of. Some blanket statements you can use when you have limited or zero knowledge about something are:

- This is something new to me. Is there anything else I should know about transactions like these? Is there anything I should be wary of?
- Is there a proper sequence to the series of transactions about to transpire which we need to observe or follow?
- Is there anything that needs to be paid, filed or complied with for this kind of transaction?
- Are there other potential scenarios not covered or identified in the agreement?
- Are there enough provisions and clauses in the agreement to protect the company, the founders, and its officers?

By asking such kind of questions, there is very little room for either party to make wrong assumptions. As I said, oftentimes, important things are left unsaid and uncovered just because the other party thought the other party knew already that is why certain questions or concerns were never taken up. The last thing that you want to hear from your service provider when something goes wrong is - "All along I thought you knew about it because you never asked."

All examples and sample computations in the book are simple in nature as the intention is to just illustrate the basic points. But please note that terms and conditions could potentially be a lot more complicated in the real setting especially as your startup grows bigger and as you get more investors. All examples also use a generic $ as currency and all amounts are merely for illustrative purposes (and are not reflective of real valuations, market prices, funding round sizes, etc.).

The book is intended for first-time founders and/or entrepreneurs who have never set up a company and/or managed the overall operations of a business before. But if you are an existing founder and still experience recurring oversights while running your company, you may also benefit from the suggested frameworks in the book. Just skip some of the chapters and sections like setting up a company, stock options and cap table computations, as you are most likely an expert on these already.

Now, before we jump to the first topic of "Setting up a Company", let's just have a quick test if you are really ready to launch your startup. Here's a checklist of some of the most important questions founders ask themselves and/or early stage investors ask founders:

- What is your value proposition?
- Is your product or service a pain killer or vitamin?
- Is the problem you are trying to address a type of pain where your target customers are willing

- to pay for it to be relieved, addressed or resolved?
- What are your TAM, SAM and SOM?
  Total Addressable Market (TAM) is the total market demand for a product/service.
  Service Available Market (SAM) is the segment of the TAM targeted by your products/services within your geographical reach.
  Service Obtainable Market (SOM) is the portion of the SAM which you can capture.

- Is the market (where you intend to play in) growing year on year? What is the estimated Compounded Annual Growth Rate (CAGR)?
- What are the macroeconomic factors that are expected to stimulate the growth of the market you are going to play in?
- How many players are in the space and similar space? Who are the key players and what are the key strengths and weaknesses of each?
- How many of these players have successfully raised funds and progressed in each funding stage (Seed, Series A, Series B and so on)?
- Is there still a big untapped opportunity in the market?
- Will you be able to disrupt the incumbents? If yes, how?
- Who are your closest competitors?
- Do you have a strong product differentiation versus your competitors? What makes you better? Why would customers shift to you? Can existing customers easily shift to your product/service, or will there be some friction or challenges for them to be able to make the shift?
- What is your moat? Is your moat defensible?

- Are there other possible substitutes or adjacent products/services that also address the same pain point/s which you are trying to solve? What and who are these?
- Does your product or service able to improve the value chain? In what way?
- What is your customer's user journey?
- What is your business model?
- What is your revenue model? How do you earn?
- Have you validated your business model by doing some tests among your target customers?
- Are your target customers willing to pay for your service/product? How did you validate it?
- What is your go-to-market strategy? How do you plan to acquire and grow your customer base?
- What is your Customer Acquisition Cost or CAC?
  There are 2 ways to measure CAC:
  One is Blended CAC which is computed by dividing your total sales & marketing costs over your registered users or customers (both paying and non-paying).
  The other is Fully-loaded CAC which is computed by dividing your total sales & marketing costs over your paying users or customers.

- What do your unit economics look like? Does it yield a positive contribution margin? Contribution Margin is computed as follows:

  Revenue per Unit
  Less: Cost of Sales per Unit

Other Direct Costs per Unit
Gross Profit
Less: Customer Acquisition Cost (CAC) per Unit

Contribution Margin

For the CAC, you can use Blended CAC or Fully Loaded CAC. The more conservative computation will be to use the Fully Loaded CAC as total sales & marketing costs are only distributed among successful sales conversions.

If you are an ecommerce startup, you can have a more detailed computation showing various levels of Profit Contribution:

Gross Sales
Less: Cost of Goods Sold

Gross Margin
Less: Payment Gateway Fees, Commissions

Profit Contribution 1 (PC1)
Less: Packaging, Delivery, other Direct Costs

Profit Contribution 2 (PC2)
Less: Customer Acquisition Cost (CAC)

Profit Contribution 3 (PC3)

- Have you done your monthly Profit & Loss (P&L) forecast? Ideally it should be done bottoms up with clear assumptions on the revenue drivers and corresponding conversion rates. Do not do a top-down approach such as basing your revenue forecasts on the assumption that you will be able to grab a certain percentage of market share and grow it year on year. Your revenue forecast should be based on the variables on how you will be able to acquire users or customers (e.g. for a B2C business, your sales assumptions could be driven by how much you spend on online ads and how many of those who clicked on the ad get converted to paying customers, and for a B2B business, sales assumptions could be driven by how many sales personnel you have, how many customers each sales staff meets per week and how many customers are they able to close within a certain period).

- Do you have your monthly cashflow forecast?
- What is your Customer Lifetime Value (CLTV)? This is the $ value of revenues derived from your user or customer for the whole duration he/she is your user or customer. For example, if an average customer buys from you an average of $20 every other month and stays with you as a customer for at least 2 years, then CLTV would be computed as $20 x 6 times per year x 2 years = $240.

As an additional metric, you can also compute your CAC payback based on your customer's CLTV. For example, your fully loaded CAC is $30. CAC payback would be computed as follows:

$240 CLTV / $30 CAC = 8 months
This means that on average, by the 8th month of a customer in your platform, the cost you spent on acquiring him/her is recovered.

- What is your estimated monthly burn? If it is not specified as gross or net burn, just assume it is gross monthly burn.

Gross monthly burn is your average monthly overhead expenses. For example, if your Total Overhead Expenses is $120,000 for a year, $120,000 divided by 12 months is $10,000 average Overhead Expenses monthly. The $10,000 amount represents your gross monthly burn.

However, if an investor asks you what your Net Cash Burn is, you need to factor in your Gross Profit into the computation. Net Cash Burn is computed as follows:

Total Overhead Expenses for the year
Less: Gross Profit
= Overhead Expenses not covered by your Gross Profit
Divided by 12 months
= Average Monthly Net Cash Burn

Let's say, your Total Overhead Expenses is $120,000 for a year and your forecasted Gross Profit for the year is $40,000, computation is as follows:
$120,000 - $40,000 = $80,000/12 months
= $6,667 Average Net Cash Burn per month

This means since your company will be able to generate some gross profit for the year, the cash you need to cover overhead expenses per month is lower which is at $6,667, and not the full monthly expenses or gross burn of $10,000 per month.

☐ How many transactions and revenues do you need to hit break-even? The easiest way to compute your break-even level is:

Ave Monthly Overhead Expenses
divided by Gross Profit Margin
= Revenues to Break-even

For example, if your Average Monthly Overhead Expenses is $10,000 and your gross margin is 20%, then:

$10,000/20% = $50,000$

This means, you need to generate at least $50,000 worth of Gross Revenues every month to be able to cover your monthly Overhead Expenses. When you exceed $50,000 in Gross Revenues, that is the only time you will start making a profit (assuming your Overhead Expenses remain at the same level).

Note: To get your Gross Margin, the formula is Gross Profit divided by Gross Revenues.

- Is the business scalable? Are you able to improve your cost efficiencies as the business scales? There are various ways to check this e.g., if your Overhead Expenses as a % of Gross Revenues is going down year on year (YoY), if the YoY growth rate of your expenses is lower than the YoY growth rate of revenues and/or gross profit, if your Ave. Revenue yield per FTE is going up YoY, etc.
- What are the most important metrics you need to track?
- How much are you raising, how do you plan to use the funds and how many months of cash runway would the funds give you?

- [ ] What milestones are you targeting to achieve in time for your next fund-raise?
- [ ] What is your long-term vision?
- [ ] How big can this business be?
- [ ] What are the potential threats and risks of your business?
- [ ] Are you a domain expert in the space you are going to play in? If not, do you have a co-founder who has domain expertise?
- [ ] Do you have a thorough understanding of the market and the value chain you will play in?
- [ ] Are there any recent news about the space or similar startups in other parts of the world that have succeeded, failed, or triggered some concerns about the business?
- [ ] Do you have the track record to execute?
- [ ] What makes you think you have what it takes to steer the company to succeed?

How well did you do? If you think you are not there yet, keep on refining what you have. Research, talk to people, conduct tests and ask for help.

*****

Key Takeaways:

- It is important to proactively lay an organized and clear foundation when you are starting a company, instead of reactively dealing with issues as they come along. There are a lot of oversights that can be avoided if you start with a proper framework. Set the right foundation at the very beginning so you can better focus on growing the company moving forward.
- Even if you hire people to do certain functions, you cannot solely depend on them and expect everything to go on smoothly. You need to

familiarize yourself with each function and regularly align with your key people. Otherwise, some things may fall through the cracks and you might find yourself in situations where your company will have financial discrepancies, tax exposure, non-compliance, filed complaints and lawsuits.
- Some oversights in accounting, finance, legal or HR may look minor, but when accumulated and compounded over time, your financials, statutory compliance and/or corporate governance could be in a big mess. All of these are important in the due diligence process and may affect the level of trust and confidence of existing shareholders, as well as prospective investors, in you.
- You cannot simply rely on your service providers (e.g. lawyers and accountants) to give you all the information you need. You have to develop the skill of asking the right questions because there are times when pieces of essential information are inadvertently omitted, or potential scenarios are not scoped, considered or foreseen, because the right questions were not asked. The best way to learn about something is to be curious and to ask the right questions.

2 SETTING UP A COMPANY

When to incorporate and where

You can easily incorporate an entity any time but one thing to keep in mind is - as soon as you incorporate, you will start incurring costs and it could be expensive. That is why you have to carefully think about the timing when to set up your company.

For some startups, they immediately incorporate two entities – one holding company and one operating entity wherein the holding company owns the operating entity. There are usually two common reasons why a holding company is set up:

(1) The operating entity is in a domicile which is not too investor-friendly, thus, the holding company is set up in a more investor-friendly domicile; and/or
(2) the long-term plan of the company is to expand to several countries and so the purpose of the holding company is to own all the operating entities in each country (subject to the foreign ownership allowed per jurisdiction).

Here are some popular domiciles for holding companies for tech startups:
- Delaware
- Singapore
- Hong Kong
- British Virgin Islands (BVI)
- Cayman Islands
- Cyprus
- Labuan

Just research on the pros and cons of each domicile once you are ready to set up a holding company. Below are some parameters you can look into when comparing various domiciles:

- Ease of forming a company (incorporation requirements, residency requirements, processing time)
- Available business types (LLC, Pte. Ltd., etc.)
- Foreign ownership restrictions
- Minimum capital requirements
- Incorporation costs
- Regulatory structure
- Tax policy
- Tax reporting requirements
- Existing tax treaties between the domicile of the holding company and where your planned operating entities would be based
- Financial reporting requirements
- Annual compliance requirements
- Administrative barriers
- Fiscal benefits
- Special incentives for startups and/or technological innovations

- Annual company maintenance costs (e.g. business registration, correspondence address, corporate secretarial fees, resident director fees, audit fee, tax agent fee, etc.)
- Stability of financial system
- Requirements to open a bank account (including checking the required minimum balance)
- Ease of doing business
- IP protection
- Dissolution requirements and costs

You can create a table plotting out the parameters you want to consider alongside your target domiciles, so it is easier to compare them apples to apples. Here's a sample table –

	Delaware	Singapore	BVI
Ease of forming a company			
Foreign ownership restrictions			
Incorporation costs			
Financial reporting requirements			
Tax Policy			
Tax Incentives, Special Incentives			
Annual compliance requirements			
Annual company maintenance costs			
<Add other parameters>			

You also must carefully think about the timing in setting up a holding company because as mentioned earlier, once you incorporate, costs would start kicking in and they could be really expensive. Imagine, if you decide to set up a holding company plus an operating entity on the onset, you need to pay for the annual maintenance expenses of two companies (not to mention the compliance work required for each entity).

Thus, if there is no need to set up a holding company yet, starting with a local operating entity is a practical decision. But what you can initially do is to at least do some pre-work on your target corporate structure. Talk to a lawyer or an expert on how to set up your target corporate structure in place (e.g., if you want a holding company to own the operating entity in the future), this way, you will have an idea on how to execute the transition (and have some peace of mind that it is something doable). This info would also be very useful when you start talking to prospective investors because some of them may likely ask you about your target corporate structure.

Putting a target corporate structure in place may sound easy but it is not that simple. It is not just about incorporating a holding company, but it requires thinking through how this new holding company would acquire the ownership of the pre-existing operating entity, or if there are any foreign ownership restrictions or required minimum paid up capital. Oftentimes, there is a required sequence of events that is why it is highly recommended that you consult a local expert. If not scoped well, you might end up incorporating unnecessary entities which cannot be used, and thus, need to be dissolved. Dissolution costs could be expensive too and the process could be time-consuming. In some domiciles, the dissolution process may even take a couple of years to get completed. Thus, make sure you have a preliminary scoping of your target corporate structure.

Important things to think about when incorporating

There are various requirements when incorporating and they differ from one country to another, but let me focus on six areas where I have seen founders usually have oversights or where they commonly make mistakes:

1. **Business Name.** Your business name does not necessarily have to be your brand name, app name or trade name. In fact, it may be wiser to make your business name different from your brand, app or trade name because sometimes, along the way, you may decide to re-brand, pivot or introduce new products or services that may not be related to the original business. Thus, having a different business name from your trade name would give you the flexibility to pivot or move forward if your initial business idea or brand name did not work, or if you expand to other product and service categories unrelated to the initial business concept.

    For some domiciles (e.g., BVI, Cayman Islands), the common practice is to purchase a shelf company for a quicker turnaround. Shelf companies are those whose names have been reserved and approved for immediate registration, or entities that have been registered already. Service providers would typically present you with a list of names of shelf companies to choose from, but alternatively, you can also incorporate a new entity if you wish to register your target company name (assuming it is available), or, you can initially buy a shelf company, then apply for an amendment in name later on.

2. **Purpose of the business.** If you are not sure what business purpose to declare when setting up your company, it is ideal to consult a lawyer. The reason is because if you inaccurately define it and end up operating outside of your declared business purpose, your company may get into serious trouble in the future. Assuming corporate documents are publicly accessible, another way is to check the declared purpose of other reputable players within the space or related space (you plan to play in) and use those as a reference, then just have a local expert validate and finalize your declared business purpose.

   Also, make sure to check if there are any regulatory restrictions and requirements given the nature of your business. For example, there are certain business categories in particular jurisdictions where there are foreign ownership restrictions, required minimum capital requirements (e.g. for financial services-related companies), required minimum capital requirements to allow 100% foreign ownership (otherwise, foreign ownership is capped at a certain threshold), special license requirements, etc. It is important to know all of these because for example, if there is a foreign ownership restriction e.g. maximum of 30%, then you can only issue up to 30% equity to foreign investors. Or if there is a minimum capital requirement that would allow 100% foreign ownership, then until you are able to raise that amount of capital required, you cannot have foreign shareholders wholly own the entity.

Some may try to do some work-around solutions – e.g., putting up a company with several layers of holding companies above the operating entity (e.g., 3 layers of holding companies above the operating entity), - but this does not work if the Ultimate Beneficial Owner/s (UBOs) or the individual/s who are in the topmost holding company is/are still foreigner/s. For some others, a foreign investor would ask a local entity or person to hold his/her/its shares in trust. However, please note that in some, or perhaps in most jurisdictions, such act constitutes a criminal offense. Please always be mindful of regulatory restrictions, do your due diligence and make sure to comply with the law.

3. **Officers.** Make sure you check if there are any citizen and residency requirements for directors and officers and to comply with it. Also, there are some jurisdictions which allow a person to hold dual roles for selected positions (e.g., a person can be both Corporate Secretary and Treasurer), but there are also certain jurisdictions that do not allow this, so know what is allowed in your chosen domicile to make sure you do not violate any of these.

4. **Corporate Compliance Paperwork.** In addition to incorporation requirements and documents, there are also some internal documents that you need to execute to support your incorporation such as Minutes and/or Resolutions on the election of the Board of Directors, officers, authorized signatories of the company, etc. The paperwork varies per domicile, and it is best to consult your Corporate Secretary

on the specific documents that need to be executed.

5. **Other Statutory and Regulatory requirements.** After incorporating, there are a handful of other things you need to apply for or comply with. Have your checklist ready. These may include things such as application for business permits, tax registration, special license/s, product registrations, etc. Find out from a local expert which ones can be done simultaneously and which ones have a required sequence (e.g., a business permit could be a pre-requisite to another requirement) so you can plan everything efficiently.

6. **Cap Table**. I chose to tackle cap table as the last item as this could be overwhelming especially for first-time founders.

    The common mistakes I have seen on cap tables are as follows:
- erroneous calculations
- realizing at a later date that one gave away too much equity
- one got full equity upfront which can no longer be taken back even if that person is unable to deliver what he/she is supposed to deliver
- not fully understanding the concept of equity dilution

Unlike making a mistake on the business name or the primary purpose of the business wherein you can file for an amendment (which is allowed in most jurisdictions), when you issue shares to someone, that's it. The only way to get back the shares is to buy them from the person which could cost a lot – assuming he/she is even willing to transfer or sell the shares to you.

Founders' Agreement

Before we discuss how to make your cap table, first things first. One of the messiest scenarios for cap tables is when one or some co-founders feel shortchanged about their equities. This is usually triggered when there is/are co-founders who is/are not delivering what they promised to deliver.

To prevent this from happening, when you start discussing about the equity split with co-founders, you have to mutually agree and be clear with the expectations and deliverables from each one, and also agree on the terms in such case as when one is unable to deliver his/her end of the bargain – because no matter how giddy you are about the company vision during the planning stage, ugly things can happen. Along the way, some co-founders may not give the same level of effort, spend as much time as other co-founders, are unable to deliver what was promised, abandon the project for another opportunity, or sometimes undergo a personal crisis which prevents them from performing their duties. Such situations have happened even among family members, best friends, and couples, and it could also happen to you.

Make sure everything you agreed upon is on paper. Think about all the possible scenarios and what are the corresponding resolutions. It can be in general principles and terms, but it can also be very specific so that there is no room for subjectivity if a situation arises e.g. if xx scenario arises within a given time frame, the defaulting party should sell yy% of his/her shares to the remaining co-founders pro-rata at $zz price. Better yet, have a lawyer draft a simple founders' agreement. This way, if any scenario does happen, it is easy to bring up the issue with your co-founders without any awkwardness. It was what was agreed upon. Nothing personal. No hard feelings.

Important items to include in a founders' agreement are:
- ownership structure
- initial capital and additional contributions
- roles and responsibilities
- equity and vesting
- salary and compensation
- management and decision-making, operating and approval rights
- budget and general guidelines for reimbursement of expenses
- taxes
- intellectual property (IP) assignment
- non-compete and confidentiality clause
- removal or departure of founders
- dissolution and termination rights
- dispute resolution

Designing your Cap Table

Now, we're ready to do your cap tables.

If you were previously overwhelmed by cap tables, now is the time to learn to like, or even love them. Computing requires only simple math. Once you understand the logic, it should be easy. You can easily compute - even on the spot - when you are talking to prospective investors.

For our simulation, let's assume you are 1 of 3 co-founders in a startup and the corresponding % ownerships you agreed upon are as follows:

Co-founders	% ownership
Mike	45%
Joey	30%
Jane	25%
Total	100%

Assuming you decide to incorporate with just the 3 of you, there are different possible scenarios depending on the capital structure allowed in your company's domicile:

With Par Value

If there is par value and each of you agreed to contribute cash pro-rata, then computation is very straightforward. Let's say you all agreed to put an initial capital of $10,000 and that the par value is $1.00/share. The initial capital table would look like this:

	Amount Paid ($1 par value)	# of Shares	% equity
Mike	$4,500	4,500	45%
Joey	$3,000	3,000	30%
Jane	$2,500	2,500	25%
Total	$10,000	10,000	100%

Another potential scenario is you all agreed that monetary contributions are not pro-rata since some co-founders are bringing in other forms of value to the company e.g., technical skills, network, etc.

Still using the same % ownership above, let's say below is what you agreed upon:

Co-founders	% ownership	Agreed contribution
Mike	45%	$6,000
Joey	30%	$3,500
Jane	25%	$2,500
Total	100%	$12,000

You decided that initial shares would be 10,000 shares and that par value is $1.

Given this, compute the number of shares of each:

Mike: 45% equity x 10,000 shares = 4,500 shares
Joey: 30% equity x 10,000 shares = 3,000 shares
Jane: 25% equity x 10,000 shares = 2,500 shares

Here's how the cap table would look like:

	# of Shares	% equity	Cost of Shares (# of shares x $1 par value)	Additional Paid-in Capital (Payment in excess of par value)	Total $ Amount
Mike	4,500	45%	$4,500	$1,500	$6,000
Joey	3,000	30%	$3,000	$500	$3,500
Jane	2,500	25%	$2,500	NA	$2,500
Total	10,000	100%	$10,000	$2,000	$12,000

Since there is par value, the total amount applied to pay for the shares is based on the par value which is $1 for each share. Thus in Mike's case, even if he paid a total of $6,000, only $4,500 is reflected as payment for his shares (4,500 shares x $1 par value=$4,500) and the balance of $1,500 ($6,000 less $4,500=$1,500) is considered a premium payment. Any payment in excess of the par value is treated as premium payment or Additional Paid-in Capital (APIC) which is reflected in the second rightmost column of the table.

By the way, percentage of ownership or equity is based on the number of shares and not on the capital contributed, so even if Mike contributed the most capital totaling $6,000, his equity is only 45% since he only owns 4,500 shares out of the 10,000 issued shares (4,500/10,000 shares=45%).

In this scenario, because the monetary contributions are not pro-rata, some of the co-founders effectively paid a higher cost per share as seen in the succeeding table:

	Total Amount Paid	# of Shares	Effective cost per share (including premium payment)
Mike	$6,000	4,500	$1.33
Joey	$3,500	3,000	$1.17
Jane	$2,500	2,500	$1.00
Total	$12,000	10,000	

In case you are in a jurisdiction where there is a minimum required number of shareholders, let's say 5, then you can add 2 more shareholders with a nominal share (1 share, if allowed). The nominal shares can be carved out from the shares of some of the co-founders so that the total shares still remain at 10,000 shares. Here's how the cap table would look like where 1 share assigned to Ben is from Mike and where 1 share assigned to Ana is from Joey:

	# of Shares	% equity
Mike	4,499	44.99%
Joey	2,999	29.99%
Jane	2,500	25%
Ben	1	.0001%
Ana	1	.0001%
Total	10,000	100.00%

Then later on, when you have enough shareholders to meet the minimum requirement, you can facilitate the transfer of the nominal shares to the corresponding co-founders who rightfully own them to clean up the cap table. Just consult your lawyer on what kind of documentation should be in place in the case of nominal shares.

There is also a possible scenario wherein there is/are co-founder/s who would not be contributing any capital. For example, the following is the agreed % equity and corresponding contributions:

Co-founders	% ownership	Agreed contribution
Mike	45%	$6,000
Joey	30%	$4,000
Jane	25%	0
Total	100%	$10,000

Since par value is required in this scenario, what you can do is come up with two (2) classes of shares with different par values e.g., $1.00 (Class A shares) and $0.01 (Class B shares), where the par value of the second class of shares is more like a symbolic amount. The example assumes $0.01 par value is allowed in a specific domicile (but note that there are also jurisdictions that have a minimum threshold for par value so please check with your local expert).

Here's how the cap table would look like using the two hypothetical par values:

	Class A shares ($1 par value)	Class B shares ($0.01 par value)	% equity	Cost of Shares ($1 par value x # of shares issued)	Additional Paid in Capital (Payt in excess of par value)	Total Amt Paid
Mike	4,500		45%	$4,500	$1,500	$6,000
Joey	3,000		30%	$3,000	$1,000	$4,000
Jane		2,500	25%	$25		$25
Total	10,000		100%	$7,525	$2,500	$10,025

Again, the percentage of ownership or equity is based on the number of shares and not on the capital contributed, so even if Mike contributed the most capital totaling $6,000, his equity is only 45% because he only owns 4,500 Class A shares out of the 10,000 total issued shares (4,500/10,000 shares=45%). While even if Jane only contributed $25 in capital, she owns 25% of the company because she owns 2,500 Class B shares out of the 10,000 total issued shares (2,500/10,000 shares=25%).

These are some possible scenarios and solutions, however, since what is allowed in each jurisdiction may differ, it is best to consult your local expert to make sure you are compliant with local regulations (as some of these may not be allowed or are not applicable to your company's domicile).

No Par Value

If **there is no par value,** the computations are pretty straightforward. Whatever capital contributions you agreed upon will be reflected as the Amount Paid. There is no concept of premium payment or Additional Paid in Capital (APIC) since there is no par value.

Let's say each of you agreed on the following % ownership with the corresponding capital contributions:

Co-founders	% ownership	Agreed contribution
Mike	45%	$4,000
Joey	30%	$5,000
Jane	25%	$1,000
Total	100%	$10,000

Given the above, here's how the cap table would look like:

	Amount Paid	# of Shares	% equity
Mike	$4,000	4,500	45%
Joey	$5,000	3,000	30%
Jane	$1,000	2,500	25%
Total	$10,000	10,000	100%

Percentage of ownership or equity is based on the number of shares and not on the capital contributed, so even if Joey contributed the most capital ($5,000 or 50% of the capital), his equity is only 30% because he only owns 3,000 shares out of the 10,000 issued shares (3,000/10,000 shares=30%).

Under this scenario, because the monetary contributions are not pro-rata, some of the co-founders effectively enjoyed lower share prices than others. Here are the effective costs of shares of each co-founder:

	Amount Paid	# of Shares	Effective cost per share
Mike	$4,000	4,500	$0.89
Joey	$5,000	3,000	$1.67
Jane	$1,000	2,500	$0.40
Total	$10,000	10,000	

Since there is no par value, the amount paid can be even a symbolic amount (e.g. $1) in exchange for any number of shares. Just check if there is any minimum required threshold in the domicile of your choice. Assuming $1 is allowed, here's another scenario where one of the co-founders' contribution is only $1 but her equity is 25%:

Co-founders	% ownership	Agreed contribution
Mike	45%	$4,000
Joey	30%	$5,000
Jane	25%	$1
Total	100%	$9,001

Given the above agreement on capital contributions and equity, here's how the cap table would look like:

	Amount Paid	# of Shares	% equity
Mike	$4,000	4,500	45%
Joey	$5,000	3,000	30%
Jane	$1	2,500	25%
Total	$9,001	10,000	100%

Since percentage of ownership or equity is based on the number of shares and not on the capital contributed, even if Jane contributed only $1 in capital, her equity is 25% because she owns 2,500 shares out of the 10,000 issued shares (2,500/10,000 shares=25%).

Cap Table Computations with Investors coming in

Let's say below is your original cap table among co-founders when you incorporated:

	Investment Amount	# of Shares	% equity
Mike	$4,500	4,500	45%
Joey	$3,000	3,000	30%
Jane	$2,500	2,500	25%
Total	$10,000	10,000	100%

Shortly after incorporating, you were able to raise a Seed round totaling $2,000,000 with a pre-money valuation of $8,000,000. Let's assume the shares to be issued are common shares and the seed investors are as follows:

Investor	Investment Amount
ABC Capital	$1,000,000
DEF Capital	$600,000
GHI Capital	$400,000
Total	$2,000,000

Here's how to compute the post-money and how much in total equity is due to investors:
Pre-money Valuation $8,000,000
Add: Funds Raised $2,000,000
Post-money Valuation $10,000,000

$2,000,000 funds raised /$10,000,000 post-money
= 20% equity

This means, in aggregate, the Seed investors in the round would own 20% of the company. But how many shares are due to each investor?

First, you need to compute the share price of the round as follows:
Pre-money Valuation $8,000,000
Divided by 10,000 Outstanding Shares
= $800 price per share

Now that you know the price per share, you can now proceed to compute each of the investor's shares:

Investor	Computation of # of shares to be issued
ABC Capital	$1,000,000 investment/ $800 price per share = 1,250 shares
DEF Capital	$600,000 investment/ $800 price per share = 750 shares
GHI Capital	$400,000 investment/ $800 price per share = 500 shares

Now that you have each of the investor's shares, plug them into the cap table. The table below shows the % Equity upon Incorporation (third column) and % Equity post-Seed (rightmost column):

	Incorporation		Post-Seed	
	# of Shares	% Equity	# of shares	% Equity
Mike	4,500	45%	4,500	36%
Joey	3,000	30%	3,000	24%
Jane	2,500	25%	2,500	20%
ABC Capital			1,250	10%
DEF Capital			750	6%
GHI Capital			500	4%
Total	10,000	100%	12,500	100%

As seen from the table above, the equity of the co-founders got diluted by 20%: Mike who originally owned 45% went down to 36%; Joey from 30% to 24%; and Jane from 25% to 20%. This is because the outstanding shares increased from 10,000 to 12,500 shares. Thus, if you divide each of the co-founder shares by 12,500 shares, the effective % ownership is now smaller e.g. for Mike, that's 4,500 shares/12,500 shares = 36% in the Seed round (versus 4,500 shares/10,000 shares = 45% during the Incorporation stage).

This is the concept of equity dilution. As you raise more funds in your startup, the equity of existing shareholders would get diluted (assuming they do not participate in the new round) because the number of outstanding shares in the company increases. Existing shareholders get diluted by the % of equity issued to the incoming investors. For example, if in your next round, the equity due to incoming investors is 10%, then each of the existing shareholders would get diluted by 10% (assuming no existing shareholder would participate in the round).

Equity dilution is something to be conscious and cautious of - if your equity becomes too small, you may have a hard time raising funds from venture capital firms because the remaining equity may not be deemed enough to motivate you to steer the company to success and to stick around through tough times. That is why you need to preserve your equity as much as you can. However, sometimes, too much equity dilution among founders could inevitably happen, thus, what some venture capital firms do is to have a stock options plan in place not just for key team members, but also for founders.

Anyway, going back to the example, let's just quickly validate if the computations we plugged into the cap table are correct.

Investor	Validation of Equity
ABC Capital	$1,000,000 investment/$10,000,000 post money valuation = 10% equity (it matches ABC's equity in the table)
DEF Capital	$600,000 investment/$10,000,000 post money valuation = 6% equity (it matches DEF's equity in the table)
GHI Capital	$400,000 investment/$10,000,000 post money valuation = 4% equity (it matches GHI's equity in the table)

It is always a smart step to do extra computations to validate if your initial computations are correct especially if there is no second pair of eyes to review your computations. You might be surprised to discover how many times you may catch erroneous figures by double-checking and triple-checking your own calculations.

In making a proper cap table, here are some important reminders:
(1) Reflect the complete names of each shareholder
(2) Show the detailed history starting from the time of incorporation in the leftmost column to the latest round in the rightmost column
(3) Each equity event or funding round should have the following columns: Investment Amount ($), # of Shares & % Equity
(4) Segregate each type of share e.g. common shares, preferred shares, etc.

However, due to the limited width of this book's page, only short aliases have been used for investors' names and some columns have been omitted such as historical details of prior rounds and column for Investment Amounts.

But here's a sample of a cap table that shows at least 2 equity events for your reference:

	Incorporation			Post-Seed			
	Investment ($)	Total Shares	% Equity	Investment ($)	New shares issued	Total shares	% Equity
Mike Smith	4,500	4,500	45%			4,500	36%
Joey Lee	3,000	3,000	30%			3,000	24%
Jane Jones	2,500	2,500	25%			2,500	20%
ABC Capital				1,000,000	1,250	1,250	10%
DEF Capital				600,000	750	750	6%
GHI Capital				400,000	500	500	4%
Total	10,000	10,000	100%	2,000,000	2,500	12,500	100.00%

Once you have raised funds externally, know that your responsibility becomes bigger as you have accepted other people's money. Investors expect to make financial returns from your company so make sure to spend the funds not just wisely, but also purposefully. Even if you raised more than enough to put into place your ideal scenario, structure or headcount, still maintain the bootstrap mindset.

For marketing, for example, do not go spending full blast just because you can now afford it. Set a budget to test first, measure the results and if it works, then you can increase your budget. If it does not work, then tweak, test, and measure again. Once something works, optimize to further improve the conversions and cost-efficiencies.

For hiring, only hire who is really needed at the right time the person is needed. Make sure there is enough work for someone to do before hiring someone full-time. You do not want to end up with a pool of staff who are not fully utilized. If your new hires start with a light load and few responsibilities, they might think that is the normal workload in the company and they may start complaining or feel overworked once it gets busier (even if the actual workload is still within reasonable range).

I have seen a lot of founders who went on a hiring frenzy after a successful round. And even if they achieved their ideal manpower headcount, topline results were never achieved, while overhead expenses ballooned due to the salaries of new hires. Before founders started realizing what was happening, the funds which were supposed to be good for 24 months' runway, got depleted in just a year. Thus, the need to fund-raise again which would further dilute the founders' equity.

*****

Key Takeaways:

- Carefully think about the timing when you need to incorporate because once you incorporate, you will start incurring costs which could be expensive.
- If you are eyeing to have a holding company, you do not have to incorporate one immediately if there is no need yet. Each entity entails corporate compliance and annual recurring costs which could be expensive. To determine if it is best to set up a holding company immediately or if it could wait at a later stage, it is best to consult a lawyer. Even if the decision is to set up at a later stage, it is important to map out the steps on how to transition to your ideal corporate structure in the future (e.g., how a newly incorporated holding company can own the existing operating entity 100% when it is time) as some prospective investors might ask these questions during fund-raising.
- Incorporation entails a lot of details – but among many details, please make sure to check regulatory restrictions and requirements depending on your company's nature of business (e.g. foreign ownership restrictions, minimum capital requirements, license requirements) and required qualifications for officers (e.g. citizenship, residency, etc.)
- For nominal shareholders who were put into place to meet compliance requirements, just check with your lawyer what documents can be executed and also find out the process on how to transfer back the nominal shares to the rightful owner/s in the future (e.g. Declaration of Trust, Deed of Assignment, etc.).

- Your company name can be different from your product, service or trade name. Having a different company name from your trade name would give you more flexibility to re-brand in the future or come up with more products and services that may be entirely different from the original product or service category you started with.
- Ignorance is not an excuse when it comes to anything that is related to the law. There are a lot of resources where you can check local regulations and requirements. Research online and ask lawyers, accountants, experts and you can even consult other startup founders.
- When you are discussing equity split with your co-founders, set clear expectations and terms. Have a written agreement on the deliverables of each one and agree on the corresponding action items and repercussions if anyone is unable to deliver what he/she promised to deliver. This would avoid unsightly, unnecessary and highly emotional conflicts in the future.
- Protect and preserve your equity as much as you can and be mindful of equity dilution. The more frequent and the more funds you raise, the smaller your equity becomes. Thus, make sure whatever funds you raise, you spend wisely and purposefully for the growth and success of the company.

3 ACCOUNTING & FINANCE

After setting up the company, founders cannot wait to kick off operations. However, some founders (especially first-time founders who have never managed the overall operations of a company before e.g., overseeing finance and HR), may overlook some important aspects of the business out of excitement.

If you are able to hire an experienced accountant who has prior experience in a similar business as your company, that's well and good. But most startups, when starting out, are on bootstrap mode. At the start, a junior accountant or bookkeeper is usually hired to save on costs. However, they may not necessarily be familiar with the nuances of certain businesses.

What commonly happens is – after hiring a bookkeeper or a junior accountant, the founder assumes that the person already knows what to do, so the founder just lets the person do the accounting and finance job, while the founder focuses on product development, sales & marketing and operations.

What kind of problems have I seen in startups when founders did this?

- The figures in the accountant's financial statements do not match the figures the founder is tracking and presenting to prospective investors and reporting to the board.
- Gross profit and unit economics cannot be properly computed because some Direct Costs were classified as Overhead Expenses by the bookkeeper.
- Customer Acquisition Costs (CAC) cannot be properly computed because online ads were classified under "Internet expenses" and lumped together with cloud hosting expenses, software subscription fees and web domain fees.
- The salaries of the Tech Team members involved in building the company's proprietary platform were not capitalized.
- There were tax penalties incurred due to the erroneous declaration of the company's income.
- There was an unusual spike in expenses for a specific month because a vendor sent a late billing covering several months of services (which the bookkeeper failed to accrue).
- Five days before the payroll period, the bookkeeper informed the founder that the company does not have enough cash to fund the payroll.
- The accountant resigned and though he turned over files, they were not complete. By the time the founder realized some files were missing, the accountant is no longer answering the company's calls and messages.

These are just some possible scenarios and consequences.

Some of these could be actually corrected by adjusting entries but this and putting your books into proper order could be really time-consuming. Not only that – imagine, if your revenues and expenses have not been properly recognized in the past months, how can you be sure about the accuracy of your computations of financial metrics? How certain are you that you have been really able to optimize your margins and costs week on week, month on month? You won't also look good to your board and prospective investors when they realize that your Audited Financial Statements do not match the reports you have presented to them before.

To help you put your accounting and financial operations in proper order right at the very beginning, below is a general checklist which you can use as a guide – but again, you have to check with your local experts (1) which ones are applicable to your jurisdiction, (2) what should be the timing of the execution (as there may be a required sequence in some jurisdictions), and (3) if there are other items not covered by this checklist. Also, in the early days of a startup, accounting and finance are typically collapsed together, but as your company grows and you hire different heads or different teams to handle each function, you can work on separating the two functions.

Sample Checklist to Organize your Accounting & Finance

- Know all your tax-related obligations.
- Know all the tax filing dates and deadlines throughout the year and make a checklist.
- Familiarize yourself with local tax laws and map out potential tax exposure for your kind of business so you'll be more careful and prevent potential problems from happening. Make sure to

- Understand the tax implications for your company's type of transactions e.g., is there VAT or DST? Are there withholding taxes or special taxes imposed when paying a local vendor versus an overseas vendor?
- Have templates for your invoice, official receipt, delivery receipt, etc. or have physical pads printed that are compliant with your tax bureau (whichever applies to your domicile).
- Open bank account/s. Ideally, one bank account for collections and one bank account for disbursements. If you foresee receiving investments and/or making cash advances in another currency, then you may also want to consider opening a foreign-denominated bank account for that purpose too. Also, do not forget to set up your payroll account.
- Decide on what accounting software to use and find out the license costs and/or monthly SaaS fees.
- Brief your accountant on the following:
  - What revenues are to be recognized
  - How you want to classify or break down your revenue streams (if there are various revenue sources)
  - Accrual policy for revenues (or when they should be recognized e.g. the month the service was rendered)
  - Accrual policy for expenses (or when they should be recognized e.g. the month when they were consumed)
  - What should be recognized as Cost of Sales (COS) and how do you want to see the breakdown (e.g., commission fee, packaging

cost, delivery cost, payment gateway fees, salaries of certain employees involved in sales and/or fulfillment of goods and services)
- How you want to classify each of the overhead expenses (some could be lumped together but think about the specific expenses you want separately classified, particularly those that you need in your metrics' computations e.g., Customer Acquisition Cost)
- What is your process when money comes in (e.g., from equity fund-raising, bridge financing, cash advances)? This could result in discrepancies in the balance sheet if the process is not established properly at the start. For an additional reference, please refer to Chapter 8 Fund-Raising and Share-Related Matters.
- What needs to be capitalized (e.g., salaries of tech team members who are building your proprietary platform as your platform could be declared as an Intangible Asset in the Balance Sheet)
- Depreciation policy of assets

☐ Accounting processes (approval process for request for payments, lead time for processing payments, etc.)

☐ Regular reports you want to see (Income statement, Cashflow Statement, Balance Sheet, etc.), your preferred report formats, the frequency of reports and who are the authorized recipients of the reports

☐ Visibility of your accountant in all your sales transactions so he/she knows what revenues to recognize for the month. For example, if you are selling in several platforms, your accountant needs to have visibility on the detailed sales transactions per platform including returns, cancelled orders, failed deliveries, etc.

- If you are engaging with a supplier, partner or any third party (e.g. consultant) and where payment is involved, always provide your accountant with a copy of the signed contract so he/she knows the terms, when is payment due and/or if it's a recurring or one-time payment.
- If anyone is using a corporate credit card, establish your company guidelines e.g., the credit card holder needs to submit to your accountant the details of his/her spending with corresponding receipts so that the accountant can properly classify each expense. There should also be a monthly cut-off date for liquidation to make sure bills are paid on time.
- Approval process of disbursements
- Collection process
- Real-time visibility of accountant to bank balances so he/she can closely monitor the cash balance. Also furnish him/her with copies of the bank statements so he/she can reconcile the bank balances periodically.
- Payroll process, cut-off dates and computations. The usual payroll-related oversight I have seen in other startups is when the accountant is not informed when new employees are onboarded. Nearing the payroll period or on the payroll date itself, the accountant is caught off-guard when a new employee follows up about his/her salary. And if there are statutory benefits, they need to be paid on time as well, as you may incur some penalties, or worse, have labor complaints filed against your company.
- Inform your accountant about any incoming funds you are expecting and/or that has been credited to the company's bank account and inform him/her how to book it – is it a loan? Shareholder's advance? Deposit for future subscription? Convertible note? Investment? And what are the corresponding terms? Furnish your accountant with the supporting documents.

- [ ] Research online and/or ask local experts on what else you need to file, apply for, pay and set up when you are starting a company.
- [ ] Explicitly inform your accountant to have an open and transparent communication with you. If he/she is not sure about how to book some transactions, he/she should not make assumptions. Rather, he/she should ask you. If there are any transactions that seem irregular, he/she should also flag you so you can both discuss what is the best way to deal with them. And yes, he/she needs to flag you even when the transactions in question involve you as you may have not noticed or realized the error/s and/or irregularities. It is important for your accountant to know that he/she can freely speak up to you and question any of the company's transactions. Honesty and transparency are very important when it comes to accounting and finance, and it is always best that problems are detected and solved at the earliest time possible.

The general rule when it comes to finance and accounting is plain and simple - you cannot expect an accountant or your finance person to know everything unless he/she is well-informed or has access to the needed data. You have to inform them and give them supporting documents (e.g. signed contracts) on anyone who needs to be paid or anything that needs to be collected or paid. He/she needs to see the detailed movements of your company's various payment channels, sales transactions, failed transactions, returns, online payments, etc. so he/she can reconcile all the figures during cut-offs.

Just in case it is your first time to oversee the finance and accounting functions and you have no idea on some of the items listed above like revenue recognition, or accruals, or capitalizing salaries of the people building your platform (so the platform can be declared as a company's Intangible Asset), you need to educate yourself. Sit down with an expert or your bookkeeper or accountant (if they are experienced) and ask him/her to explain to you the importance of each of the items listed above and then, when you fully understand everything, you can make the decisions and be able to finalize the processes.

Finally, make sure that for every process you design, there are control measures in place for check and balance. No one should have full control of transactions and funds so that if anyone does something erroneously – whether unintentionally or maliciously - there is a way for the company to detect it. For example, ideally, the person handling collections and disbursements should be two different individuals, otherwise, a person would have control on both the inflow and outflow of the company's money.

Another critical area for finance and accounting which you need to be mindful of is when your bookkeeper or accountant leaves. You need to have a thorough checklist in place for the turnover to ensure that you have everything you need before he/she leaves. Because after you sign the employee's clearance papers and release one's final pay, he/she no longer has obligations to your company. Some ex-employees may still be responsive and helpful even after leaving the company because of a good relationship you were able to establish with them, but it is not always the case. Thus, take it upon yourself to be in charge in proactively identifying what you need to secure from a resigning personnel instead of just relying on what he/she turns over to you. You need to do this within the time he/she is still employed with your company to be fair to him/her, so that he/she can move on to his/her next endeavor after his/her employment with your company ends.

A proper turn-over would mutually benefit both parties as the company is able to function with minimal or no disruption (after all, no one should be indispensable) and the resigning accountant can also move on and focus on his/her new job.

Below is a sample checklist which you can use as a guide – but again, this is not exhaustive and some items may not be applicable to your jurisdiction. But what is important is to make sure you have something like this in place.

Sample Turnover Checklist for a Resigning Accountant

- Latest financial statements – Income Statement, Balance Sheet and Cashflow Statement. Review each one if you have any questions. If the replacement accountant will use the same accounting software, disable your resigning accountant's access on his/her last reporting day. If you plan to use a different software moving forward, ask the resigning accountant to extract soft copies of all accounting files and financial statements.
- Manual Books of Accounts and Journals (if any)
- Retrieval of tax filing returns from day 1 of incorporation - these are needed for audit and for any future inspection by the tax bureau
- Retrieval of the online tax filing access (please also make sure to update the authorized person/s and/or email addresses associated with your company and registered in your tax bureau)
- Summary of all the accountant's online access so you can plan the deactivation of his/her account/s and the addition of the new personnel in charge.

- List of the contact details of suppliers, vendors, partners, service providers (e.g. auditor, tax agent) and clients he/she regularly corresponds with
- Schedule of recurring transactions
- Templates, booklets or pads of the Company's Invoice, Statements of Account, Official Receipt, Delivery Receipt, etc. (if applicable)
- Original proofs of payment for statutory benefits
- Disbursement Files e.g. Requests for Payments, Vouchers, ORs issued by vendors, monthly disbursement schedule
- Account Receivables' Files e.g. Invoice Files, Statements of Account, monthly collection schedule, etc.
- Past years' Audited Financial Statements (AFS)
- Original business documents in case they are being safekept by your accountant e.g. Certificate of Incorporation, By-laws, Business Permit, etc.
- List of pending items, latest status of each pending item (including email threads or correspondences) and endorsement to corresponding contact persons.
- Other Accounting Files
- Bank-related details and documents such as:
  - Bank Account details
  - Online Banking Access - please make sure you remove your accountant's access and change password/s right after the turnover so your accountant won't be able to access the account anymore
  - Bank passbooks and checkbooks
  - Bank statements
  - Bank's contact details
  - Process on how to remove your accountant as an authorized person in your bank account/s and how to assign a new authorized person.

- ☐ Scope other items that need to be added to the list depending on what is applicable to your domicile and the nature of your business.

As a final note - no matter how busy you are, review your finances. Every cent counts. You have to treat your money and your investor's money like all of it were your own. And even if you highly trust the people who handle your finance and accounting, there is no better and more honest financial steward than you.

*****

Key Takeaways:

- Just because one is a bookkeeper or an accountant, do not assume that he/she already knows everything that needs to be done in your business. Perhaps, he/she may know, but how about you? If you have never overseen accounting and finance functions yet, it is time to learn and educate yourself. The best way to prevent financial-related problems from happening is to sit down with a local expert, or your bookkeeper or accountant (if they have prior experience). Going over the suggested checklist here would be a good start.
- You need to set up your accounting books properly from the very beginning to have accurate financials.
- You need to inform your bookkeeper or accountant about all the company's transactions because he/she would not be able to know the details and terms if he/she does not have visibility in some of the transactions (particularly if you

have a lot of online sales channels).
- You need to carefully design your processes to ensure that there are check and balance measures and that they are fool-proof from possible fraudulent activities triggered by insiders.
- Have an open and transparent communication with your accountant. You should explicitly inform him/her that he/she can ask questions if he/she is not sure about some transactions or when he/she detects some irregular transactions – even if you have approved the transactions - as you may have not noticed or realized the error/s and/or irregularities. It is important for your accountant to know that he/she can freely speak up to you and question any of the company's transactions.
- Even if you highly trust the people who handle your finance and accounting, remember that there is no better and more honest financial steward than you.

4 HR

When one is just starting a company and trying to minimize overhead costs, HR is a function that is commonly absorbed by the founders themselves or by another senior manager, or occasionally, outsourced to a consultant. All of these are ways to save on costs, however, if HR processes are not properly established, there are things that may get overlooked and you might end up with problems such as:

- Delayed processing of payroll
- Wrong computation of consultant fees
- Wrong computation of overtime pay
- Erroneous tracking of leave credits
- Delayed filing and payment of statutory benefits (because the company allowed some employees to start working even if they have failed to submit some employment requirements)
- Impending threat of a labor case from a disgruntled employee or worse, a filed labor complaint e.g., illegal termination
- Resigned employees still have access to shared

folders and drives, corporate accounts and official chat groups

But your startup does not have to go through the same painful experiences because most of these potential problems could be avoided if only you spend some time thinking about the processes and tools to organize your HR function.

Here's a checklist which you can use as a guide, then just edit, and build on it, depending on the local requirements of your domicile.

Sample Checklist in Organizing your HR

- ☐ Know all employer-related obligations and familiarize yourself with the local labor law.
- ☐ Determine what are the minimum employee benefits required by law and make sure you comply. Since the company is not yet profitable during early days, be wary of granting benefits that are convertible to cash such as leaves (unless cash conversion is required by law) as these could accumulate as liabilities over time.
- ☐ Understand the differences of the various types of engagement e.g. full-time employee versus a contractual employee versus a consultant, and make sure that your contracts reflect the proper terms for each (e.g. statutory benefits, taxes). Unclear or vague language may sometimes be misconstrued and could be a potential source of labor complaints.
- ☐ Have ready templates for job offers, employment contracts, consultancy contracts, etc. Have your contract templates reviewed by an experienced HR personnel and/or lawyer to be sure language is accurate. Once you have the approved

templates, it should be easy for any person handling HR to draft contracts every time there is a new hire.
- Have your pre-employment checklist – what are the things you would require new hires to submit e.g. clearance from past employer, photocopy of birth certificate, valid government ID, transcript of records, SSS number, etc.
- Design your onboarding process and have a checklist e.g. creation of an employee's email address, wi-fi access, door security access, provision for laptop, etc.
- Coordinate with Accounting in setting up the payroll account and discuss the following:
  - Payroll process
  - Cut-off dates
  - Payroll Computations
  - Attendance reports
  - Policy on leaves and leaves' tracking
  - Process for resigning employees e.g. release of final pay
- Coordinate with Accounting if you are engaging with consultants. Provide your accountant with the signed contract so he/she knows what has been agreed upon e.g. if the amount is gross or net, what taxes are to be withheld and paid, when is payment due, etc.
- Have a system in place for properly organizing employee files.
- Think about your performance feedback and appraisal process.
- Have an exit process for resigning employees – turnover of files, retrieval of company assets, clearance, disabling and deactivation of all the accounts associated with the resigning employee, removal of resigning employee from all official chat groups and channels, etc.

- Consult a local expert about other HR-related matters e.g., termination of an employee and retrenchment, as conditions and requirements may differ from one country to another. You need to carefully educate yourself on these things so you know what you are allowed to do within the labor code of your domicile. Sometimes out of frustration on a specific employee, you might find yourself making rash decisions that may be in violation of the labor code so make sure you know your local laws well.
- Research online and ask local experts on what else you need to know, do and comply with as an employer in your domicile.

The potential repercussions of oversights on departing employees could be serious especially if the oversights include forgetting to retrieve important files, failing to retrieve the super admin access to an online account and not deactivating or removing the person's access to confidential files or channels. To prevent such oversights, here's a sample checklist which you can edit and build on (if the resigning employee is from Accounting or Finance, please refer to the sample checklist in Chapter 3):

Sample Turnover Checklist for a Resigning Employee

- Retrieve all company files and documents
- Ask him/her to turn over all pending items and supporting files and/or latest email threads on these items (and also request that he/she endorse you to the people he/she corresponds with)
- List of the person's external office contacts and their contact details

- [ ] Retrieve all company-owned equipment and assets that were assigned to the person e.g. laptop, ID, HMO card, etc.
- [ ] Make sure to inform third-party vendors to terminate the resigning employee's subscription to employee benefits e.g. HMO plan
- [ ] Deactivate the employee's email address
- [ ] Deactivate the employee's door access code
- [ ] Disable and deactivate the access of the person in all systems, apps, accounts and websites such as:
    - company's social media accounts e.g. Linkedin, Facebook, Instagram (if he/she has admin access)
    - shared folders and drives e.g. Google Drive, Dropbox
    - company domains/websites e.g. GoDaddy
    - third party apps (used by Tech, Sales & Marketing, HR, etc.) e.g. Canva, Salesforce
    - other corporate accounts

  Ideally, you need to keep track of all the apps and tools that the company is using because with the continuous introduction of new technologies, the company will most likely keep on adding new apps and tools. There is a high chance that some accounts used by the company will be forgotten or omitted if your checklist does not detail each and every account used per category and per team.
- [ ] If files of the resigning employee are in a shared drive, make arrangement for the transfer of ownership of the files before terminating his/her account
- [ ] Change all the passwords to the accounts where the person had previous access to
- [ ] Remove the person from all official chat groups and channels e.g. Slack, Telegram

- ☐ Update the company website and remove any references to the employee if the resigning employee is featured under the Team Page .
- ☐ Update the company's list of signatories if the resigning employee is an authorized signatory
- ☐ Scope other items applicable to the nature of your business and local setting

If you only take some time to understand and put all of these in place as you are starting your company, you will be able to prevent a lot of oversights and mistakes from happening, or better yet, save your company from having labor cases or having unauthorized access to your company's confidential info and online assets.

*****

Key Takeaways:

- If you are not familiar with your local labor laws, educate yourself. It does not matter if you hire an HR person who will handle the function, you still need to know as you might find yourself making rash decisions in the future which may get you into trouble for violating your labor code.
- Checklists come in handy in organizing your HR processes. Have one for pre-employment, onboarding and resigning employees. Regularly update your checklists especially the one for resigning employees (as your startup continues to try new online tools and apps). This way, you can revoke all online access of resigning employees and preserve the integrity of your company's files, data and communication.
- Do not entirely rely on a resigning employee to

scope what he/she needs to turn over. Sometimes out of excitement to start a new chapter in one's career, the resigning employee's turnover is not complete. You need to make it your responsibility (or the immediate supervisor's responsibility) to retrieve all that the company needs to retrieve from a resigning employee so that everyone can properly move on after an employee's departure.

The Organized Startup

5 LEGAL & CORPORATE COMPLIANCE

In your startup journey, there will be a lot of legal paperwork and corporate compliance. Legal documents are often long and use jargons that can be intimidating. And because they are lengthy and oftentimes not easy to understand, you will be tempted to rely on your lawyer's assessment.

Here's an important piece of advice - even if your lawyer says everything looks good, you have to take it upon yourself to understand everything. If you find some provisions and clauses beyond your comprehension, ask your lawyer what they mean and what are they for because each clause in a contract is there for a reason.

When it comes to legal documents, always remember that there is no such thing as a stupid question. Not asking clarifying questions when you do not understand something is what is stupid. It is always in your best interest to fully understand everything in an agreement. What you don't want to happen is for some clause that you did not try to understand gets triggered which has serious consequences on your company and/or you. It is in being curious and in asking questions that you are able to understand better and learn best.

Some of the more common legal documents you will come across in your startup journey include the following:

- **Non-disclosure agreement (NDA).** This can be one-way (if only one party is disclosing confidential information) or two-way (if both parties are disclosing confidential information).
- **Term Sheet.** This is usually a non-binding document that outlines the proposed terms due from each party on a certain transaction e.g., bridge financing, fund-raising.
- **Convertible Note.** This is a form of agreement wherein an investor lends money to a startup (with interest and a maturity period), and the investor has an option to convert the debt (and interest) into equity based on some pre-agreed terms and trigger conditions.
- **Subscription Agreement.** This is a form of contract wherein a company agrees to sell a certain number of shares at a specific price, and in return, the subscriber (the investor) promises to buy the shares at the pre-agreed price.
- **Shareholders' Agreement.** This is a document signed by a company's shareholders that outlines shareholders' rights and obligations, the operations of the business and its decision-making process. It is important for a founder to take note of what the company committed in this agreement and to make sure they are properly observed and exercised.
- **Deed of Adherence.** If there is an existing Shareholders' Agreement already but a company adds more shareholders, the new shareholders have to sign a Deed of Adherence which basically

states that the new shareholders agree to the terms of the company's existing Shareholders' Agreement.
- **Stock Purchase Agreement / Deed of Assignment / Deed of Sale** (or a similar document applicable to your domicile). These are forms of agreement wherein a shareholder agrees to sell a certain number of a company's shares at a specific price, and in return, a buyer promises to buy the shares at the pre-agreed price.

Corporate compliance, on the other hand, consists of paperwork that you are duty-bound to circulate, route, secure approval, execute and/or file such as notices, waivers, minutes of the meeting, secretary's certificates, and board resolutions. It is probably one of the least favorite areas of founders, but it must be done - no matter what - because these are the documents surrounding a company's major decisions and transactions such as election of officers, capital raise, issuance of new shares, assignment of authorized signatories, share transfers, among many others.

To know what your duties surrounding corporate compliance are, you need to familiarize yourself with your articles of incorporation, by-laws and shareholders' agreement (if any) and other corporate documents applicable to your domicile.

Typically, your Corporate Secretary is the one who takes the lead in drafting and executing the paperwork. However, your Corporate Secretary would not know your company's ongoing transactions unless you inform him/her. Thus, it would help if you have a checklist on what would constitute sending out notices to your shareholders and/or board, securing approval from your shareholders and/or board, filing paperwork in government bureaus and payment of statutory obligations (e.g., tax payments) so you won't violate any of these or be negligent in complying.

Make an inventory of all the corporate actions subject to board and/or shareholder approval by putting them all in one checklist so you have a quick reference. Here are some common items:

Sample Checklist of Corporate Actions subject to Board and/or Shareholder Approval

(Just add/remove items depending on what is specified in your by-laws and Shareholders' Agreement.)

- ☐ Annual Shareholders' Meeting – make sure to set it as a recurring item in your calendar. This usually entails distributing notices and the company's latest minutes within a certain number of days before the Annual Shareholders' Meeting date. Your Corporate Secretary can do all the paperwork, but it does not hurt if you remind your Corporate Secretary weeks in advance (in case it slips his/her mind).
- ☐ Amendment/s to the Articles of Incorporation or By-laws
- ☐ Entering into any agreements that could be of material importance (e.g. license contracts, customer contracts, vendor contracts, consulting agreements, lease agreements, etc.)
- ☐ Issuance of dividends
- ☐ Borrowing or lending money
- ☐ Annual budget
- ☐ Hiring and/or terminating senior management (or amending terms of their employment)
- ☐ Adopting new employee benefit plans
- ☐ Sale or other distribution of company assets
- ☐ Anything that is equity-related such as:

- Increase in authorized capital
- Issuance of shares
- Issuance of new type of shares
- Conversion of notes or shareholder advances to equity
- Approval of stock options, stock grants or any stock warrant/s
- Transfer of shares (whether the transfer is to a related or unrelated party)

Anything equity-related usually requires notices sent to shareholders and signed waivers since existing shareholders have the inherent right to participate in any equity-related transaction pro-rata to their shareholding. That is why it's mandatory to closely coordinate with your Corporate Secretary regarding any share-related transaction to make sure you do not violate any shareholder rights and to ensure that you comply with all the required filings and payments (e.g., tax payments). Sample checklists on some share-related transactions can be found in Chapter 7 Stock Options and Chapter 8 Fund Raising and Share-Related Matters.

- [ ] Entering into a contract with a related party
- [ ] Election of officers
- [ ] Assignment or updating of authorized signatories
- [ ] Appointment of the company's auditor
- [ ] Opening of a bank account
- [ ] Investment in a company
- [ ] Dissolution or winding up of the company
- [ ] Scope other items specified in your articles, by-laws, shareholders' agreement and other corporate documents, and take note of all the prescribed period required per type of transaction.

Similar to a change in your accountant or your HR person, a change in your Corporate Secretary requires meticulous scoping of what materials and files need to be retrieved. Here's a sample checklist as a guide – please make sure to retrieve all the original hard copies (where applicable) and soft copies (for those electronically-executed) from your outgoing Corporate Secretary:

Sample Checklist of Files to be Retrieved from an Outgoing Corporate Secretary

- ☐ Signed Minutes
- ☐ Signed Board or Directors' Resolutions
- ☐ Signed Secretary's Certificates
- ☐ Signed Waivers
- ☐ Signed Subscription Agreements
- ☐ Signed Shareholders' Agreement
- ☐ Signed Deeds of Adherence to the Shareholders' Agreement
- ☐ Signed Stock Purchase Agreements
- ☐ Stock Transfer Book
- ☐ Any other share-related documents
- ☐ Share Certificates
- ☐ Company Seal
- ☐ Receiving copies of filed documents in government bureaus
- ☐ Other Corporate documents safe-kept by the Corporate Secretary

Reading legal documents, doing paperwork and routing them for signature can be time-consuming but all of these have to be done. They are also a form of check and balance as it shows proof that everyone who should know about the company's most important decisions and transactions have been properly informed and have given their approval.

Most of these documents are also required in your annual audit and are typically required as part of the due diligence process when you raise funds. Your startup must be in proper order because if you cannot get it in order while it's still small, how can you manage it when it grows bigger?

*****

Key Takeaways:

- No matter how long and difficult it is to read legal documents, carefully read and understand each provision. If you do not understand something, ask your lawyer. There is no such thing as a stupid question. Not asking clarifying questions when you do not understand something in a legal document is what is stupid. It is in being curious and asking the right questions that will make you sharper.
- Make an inventory of all the commitments the company made to its shareholders – check your articles, by-laws, shareholders' agreement, term sheets, side letters, etc. – and create a checklist. You may think that it's just paperwork for formality, but those are serious rights and obligations you promised to your investors. Failure to deliver them may strain your relationship with your shareholders, affect your integrity or result to a breach of contract with serious repercussions.
- Always inform your Corporate Secretary about decisions and transactions that are included in your commitment to shareholders so he/she can help you prepare and route the paperwork for

compliance.
- Corporate compliance may be time-consuming but it is a form of check and balance. It is proof that everyone who should know about the company's most important decisions and transactions have been properly informed and have given their approval.

6 MASTER DATA ROOM

A Data Room typically comes into a founder's mind only when a startup is fund-raising because it is required by investors as part of the due diligence process. But a Data Room that is properly organized (right from the start of the company's operations) could be a powerful resource for a founder even when there is no fund-raising activity.

As you go about managing the company, you will find yourself revisiting past agreements or trying to recall certain details of past transactions (whether it's about a sales transaction, or the terms of your last convertible note, or your operating expenses for a particular period, or double-checking the terms of your current lease contract). The only way to validate such details is to dig up past email threads and/or ask the persons in charge to look for the pertinent files (both of which could be time-consuming). Instead of repeatedly asking your accountant, or your HR personnel, or your Corporate Secretary for any of these documents, the smarter thing to do is to set up a Master Data Room so you and the company's key people have access to your company's most important documents anytime, anywhere.

The best time to set up a Master Data Room is at the start of your startup journey so you can instill the discipline to organize files as they are finalized and executed (but if you have an existing company already, it is also never too late to organize one). Have a framework in place and start populating it with content. The objective is to develop the habit of saving and organizing all your company's important files in one Master Data Room as each file is completed. This way, you do not waste time searching for documents in your past emails or messages or bothering colleagues to search for you. Everything will be in one repository and files should be easy to find and to retrieve if they are properly organized and labeled.

To set up your Master Data Room, you can use any cloud-based platform that you trust like Dropbox and Google Drive. There are also other options like Digify and SecureDocs.

Your Master Data Room should contain scanned copies of your corporate documents, copies of your signed documents and contract templates. You can organize related documents in folders and sub-folders for easier retrieval. Below is a sample organizational folder structure (where main folders are arranged alphabetically):

Sample Folder Structure for a Master Data Room

- Audited Financial Statements
- Capitalization Table
- Client Contracts
- Convertible Notes
- Corporate Documents
    - Articles of Incorporation / By-laws (or whichever is applicable in your

jurisdiction)
- ♦ Business Profile
- ♦ Certificate of Incorporation
- ♦ Corporate Structure (if you have more than 1 entity)
- ♦ Registry of Directors (ROD) & Registry of Members (ROM) (or whichever is applicable in your jurisdiction)
- ♦ Tax Registration
- ☐ Employee Stock Options (ESOP)
- ☐ Financials
  - ♦ Year-to-date: P&L, Balance Sheet, Cashflow Statement
  - ♦ Projections: P&L, Balance Sheet, Cashflow Statement
  - ♦ Financial Model
  - ♦ Use of Funds
- ☐ HR
  - ♦ Consultancy Agreement Template
  - ♦ Employment Agreement Template
  - ♦ Organizational Structure
  - ♦ Biodata or CVs of Founders
  - ♦ Biodata or CVs of the Management Team
- ☐ Intellectual Property Documents
  - ♦ Trademarks
  - ♦ Patents
- ☐ Lease Contract/s
- ☐ Marketing Materials
- ☐ Market Research
- ☐ Memorandum of Agreements (MOAs)
- ☐ Minutes and Resolutions
- ☐ Non-Disclosure Agreements
- ☐ Promissory Notes
- ☐ Shareholders' Agreement
  - ♦ Shareholders Agreement

- ♦ Deeds of Adherence
- ♦ Amended Shareholders' Agreement (if any)
- ☐ Subscription Agreements /Investment Agreements
- ☐ Share Certificates & Receiving Copies of Share Certificates
- ☐ Stock Purchase Agreements / Share Transfer Documents (e.g. Deeds of Sale, Deeds of Assignment)
- ☐ Technology
- ☐ Term Sheets
- ☐ Vendor Contracts
- ☐ Voting Agreements
- ☐ Add any other folder/sub-folders applicable to your business

To facilitate quick search and retrieval of documents, develop a descriptive file-naming convention. The relevant words you use in creating filenames would make them appear in search results. Think of the words you put in your filenames as the possible keywords you will type when searching for them.

Here are some examples of descriptive file name formats:

For Audited Financial Statements:
Company name_AFS_<financial year of audit>

For convertible notes:
CN_<lender's name>_<amount>_<month_year>

For non-disclosure agreements:
NDA_<company name>_date

For resolutions:
Resolution_<decision/s approved>_<month_year>

For share certificates:
Share Certificate_<certificate no.>_<shareholder's name>_<# of shares>_<date>

For subscription agreements:
Subscription_<investor's name>_<investment amount>_<month_year>

Once you develop the habit of properly naming files and immediately saving and organizing them into your data room, everything should be easy. Any time you need to refresh your mind or validate a past transaction or detail, no worries. You can easily retrieve and check the relevant file. No time wasted searching through past email threads or chat messages or bothering colleagues to look for documents.

When it's time to raise funds, there is no need to cram either. You could easily set up a customized Data Room for each of your prospective investors since you have all the important files of your company in one repository. You can quickly duplicate the relevant folders needed to be shared depending on an investor's requirements. But if there is no list given, here's a sample guide on what you can include in your Investor Data Room:

Sample Folder Structure for an Investor Data Room

- Audited Financial Statements
- Capitalization Table
- Convertible Notes
- Corporate Documents
    - Articles of Incorporation / By-laws (whichever is applicable in your jurisdiction)
    - Business Profile

- Certificate of Incorporation
- Corporate Structure (if you have more than 1 entity)
- Registry of Directors (ROD) & Registry of Members (ROM) (whichever is applicable in your jurisdiction)
- Tax Registration
- Employee Stock Options (ESOP)
- Financials
  - Year-to-date: P&L, Balance Sheet, Cashflow Statement
  - Projections: P&L, Balance Sheet, Cashflow Statement
  - Financial Model
- HR
  - Headcount
  - Organizational Structure
- Intellectual Property Documents
  - Trademarks
  - Patents
- Marketing Materials
- Market Research
- Minutes and Resolutions
- Promissory Notes
- Shareholders' Agreement
- Subscription Agreements / Investment Agreements
- Stock Purchase Agreements / Share Transfer Documents
- Technology
- Voting Agreements

You may set the access rights of prospective investors to read-only, however, for financial projections, it is best that you provide them with editable files (e.g., Excel or Numbers file) so it is easier for them to check formulas, understand your assumptions and analyze your projections.

After the due diligence process, do not forget to revoke the prospective investor's access to the Data Room (or set an expiration date on the user access if the feature is available in your chosen platform).

*****

Key Takeaways:

- Set up your Master Data Room as you are just starting your company. Develop the habit of saving and organizing all of the company's important files in your data room as each document is finalized and executed. Properly label each folder and sub-folder in the Master Data Room so you can easily trace the right folder when searching or saving files.
- Develop a descriptive file-naming convention – think of the keywords you will type when searching for specific files. The right descriptive words in the filename would facilitate quick search and retrieval of files within the data room. No time wasted searching through past email threads or messages or bothering colleagues to look for the needed documents.
- With a properly organized Master Data Room in place, you can easily set up a customized Data Room for each of your prospective investors when fund-raising time comes. Since you have all the important files of your company in one repository, you can quickly duplicate the relevant folders needed to be shared depending on an investor's requirements. After the completion of

the due diligence process, do not forget to revoke the prospective investor's access to the Data Room (or set an expiration date for the user access if there's an available feature in your chosen platform).

7 EMPLOYEE STOCK OPTIONS

Employee Stock Options are a type of incentive that gives employees the right to buy shares in the company at a specified price within a prescribed period of time. They are typically used to attract, motivate and retain talented employees. By offering equity to new hires, a startup can conserve cash while attracting talents who are willing to commit to the company and help it scale and achieve its vision.

Stock options matter to employees because if the startup's valuation continues to exponentially grow year on year, an employee's equity could result to a huge financial upside in the future. And just like the founders and investors, once some employees own equity, it would also be in their best interest to make the startup succeed.

There are 4 components that you need to remember about Employee Stock Options: Vesting, Cliff, Exercise Price & Exercise Period.

Here's an illustration on how stock options work:
- John Doe is an employee of XYZ Co.

- As part of his package, he was given an option to buy 36,000 shares of XYZ's common shares at $0.10 per share.
- The options are subject to a three-year vesting period (shares equally divided per year or equivalent to 12,000 shares per year) with one year cliff vesting. This means that John has to stay employed with XYZ for at least one year before he gets the right to exercise the first 12,000 share options. Then the balance of 24,000 share options will vest at the rate of 1/24 a month over the next 24 months (or 2 years) of John's employment (completing the 3-year vesting period). Here's how John's vesting schedule would look like:

John's employment	Shares vested for the period	Cumulative shares vested
Month 12	12,000	12,000
Month 13	1,000	13,000
Month 14	1,000	14,000
Month 15	1,000	15,000
Month 16	1,000	16,000
Month 17	1,000	17,000
Month 18	1,000	18,000
Month 19	1,000	19,000
Month 20	1,000	20,000
Month 21	1,000	21,000
Month 22	1,000	22,000
Month 23	1,000	23,000
Month 24	1,000	24,000
Month 25	1,000	25,000
Month 26	1,000	26,000
Month 27	1,000	27,000
Month 28	1,000	28,000
Month 29	1,000	29,000

Month 30	1,000	30,000
Month 31	1,000	31,000
Month 32	1,000	32,000
Month 33	1,000	33,000
Month 34	1,000	34,000
Month 35	1,000	35,000
Month 36	1,000	36,000
Total: 3 years	**36,000**	

- If John resigns from XYZ or he is terminated for a cause before his first year of employment, John won't get any of the options because there is a one-year cliff.
- Once his options are vested, they become exercisable, and John has the option to buy them at the pre-agreed price which is $0.10 per share.
- Let's say John leaves at the end of Month 30 of his employment, his total shares vested would be 30,000 shares (as illustrated in the table).
- If after three years John is still employed at XYZ, all his 36,000 options would be fully vested.
- Assuming John exercised his options and buys all 36,000 shares, the cost would be $3,600 (36,000 shares x $0.10 = $3,600).
- If XYZ becomes successful and does an IPO, where let's say the share price traded at $10 per share, the worth of John's 36,000 shares which he bought for only $3,600 would now be worth $360,000 (36,000 shares x $10 per share).

As for the exercise period, this is the period wherein an employee can still exercise his right to the vested shares. Some companies limit it within the employment period of the employee and for some, they give a prescribed period beyond the termination date of employment e.g. 60 to 90 days from the end date of employment or sometimes, even several years from the employment date. If an employee is not able to exercise his/her right within the prescribed period, then the options get forfeited.

The above example is a simple scenario to illustrate how stock options work. There could be other possible terms and conditions e.g. triggers when vesting can be accelerated, option of the company to buy back the shares when an employee resigns, among many others.

There are also some jurisdictions that require a formal filing of an Employee Stock Options Plan (ESOP) with a government bureau, so please check what is applicable to your domicile. Also, please be mindful if your company has foreign ownership restrictions – if you have already reached the maximum limit of foreign ownership allowed in your entity, this means that you cannot have ESOP recipients who are not local citizens.

Now that you have a general idea on how stock options work, the next set of questions you might have are - how do you compute your stock options pool and how does it affect the cap table?

Let's say this is your existing cap table:

	Outstanding shares	% Equity
Mike	4,500	36%
Joey	3,000	24%
Jane	2,500	20%
ABC Capital	1,250	10%
DEF Capital	750	6%
GHI	500	4%

Capital		
Total	12,500	100.00%

Now, you got approval from shareholders and the Board to allocate 10% for your Employee Stock Options Plan (ESOP). Typically, it can range from 5 to 20% (10% is more common), but the final percentage depends on what you collectively (shareholders and board) decide since options, once exercised, would have a dilutive effect.

Given the 10% approved employee stock options, here's how to compute your stock options' allocation or pool:

Current Outstanding Shares 12,500
Divided by (100% less 10%) or 90%
= 13,889 Total Shares (this represents the total shares including the stock options' pool)
Note: The current outstanding shares is divided by 90% because 12,500 should represent 90% (while the stock options' pool should represent 10%.)

13,889 Total shares (including stock options)
Less 12,500 current Outstanding Shares
= 1,389 shares for stock options pool

To validate:
1,389 shares for stock options / 13,889 Total shares = 10%

Now that you know how many shares are in your stock options' pool, let's plug in the figure into the cap table and see the impact on the shareholding:

	Pre-ESOP		Post-ESOP	
	Shares	% Equity	Shares (including Stock Options)	% Equity
Mike	4,500	36.00%	4,500	32.40%
Joey	3,000	24.00%	3,000	21.60%
Jane	2,500	20.00%	2,500	18.00%
ABC Capital	1,250	10.00%	1,250	9.00%
DEF Capital	750	6.00%	750	5.40%
GHI Capital	500	4.00%	500	3.60%
ESOP			1,389	10.00%
Total	12,500	100.00%	13,889	100.00%

Important Note: *Due to the limited page width of the book, some columns have been omitted such as historical details of prior rounds and column for Investment Amounts.*
To make a proper cap table, please make sure to:
(1) Reflect the complete names of each shareholder.
(2) Show the detailed history starting from the time of incorporation in the leftmost column to the latest round in the rightmost column.
(3) Each equity event or funding round should have the following columns: Investment Amount ($), # of Shares & % Equity.
(4) Segregate each type of share e.g. common shares, preferred shares.

As you can see, all shareholders would be diluted by 10% if all of the stock options would be exercised.

Now that you have a stock options' pool, just make sure you abide by what you, your shareholders and the Board have agreed relating to the awarding of the shares, the recipients and the terms and conditions. You also need to have a tracker to make sure how many shares have been allocated to employees already so that at any time, you know the balance that is left unallocated. If someone resigns before the cliff vesting or before the full vesting period, then there would be some shares that would go back to the pool (assuming this is the term agreed upon in the Plan). That is why a tracker for your stock options pool is very important – so you know how many share options are still available, at any given time, for the talent pool you want to attract, motivate, reward and retain.

Here's a sample of a simple tracker as a guide but you can further customize the columns depending on what you want to track.

Employee	Start of Vesting	Completion of Vesting	Total Stock Options
Brian Smith	*<mm-dd-yyyy>*	*<mm-dd-yyyy>*	100
Ana Chan	*<mm-dd-yyyy>*	*<mm-dd-yyyy>*	200
Vince Jones	*<mm-dd-yyyy>*	*<mm-dd-yyyy>*	100
Camille Ty	*<mm-dd-yyyy>*	*<mm-dd-yyyy>*	200
Ema Ross	*<mm-dd-yyyy>*	*<mm-dd-yyyy>*	300
Total allocated			900
Total ESOP allocation			1,389
Balance (still unallocated)			489

If you prefer a more detailed table, additional columns that may be useful are:
- Number of vested shares to-date
- Number of options exercised to-date
- Exercise price per employee (if there are varying exercise prices)
- End of exercise period

- Employment Status of Employee
- Number of Freed up Shares (in case vesting is terminated so you can add these shares back to the Share Options' pool – assuming this is what has been agreed up in your Stock Options Plan)
- Other trigger points and scenarios outlined in your Stock Options Plan.

Once you have an Employee Stock Options Plan (ESOP) in place, you also need to disclose this to your prospective investors and incorporate it in the computation of cap tables so that incoming investors would know what their fully diluted % equity post-ESOP (more on this in Chapter 8 Fund-raising and Other Share-related Matters).

Finally, since this is equity-related, you need to closely work with your Corporate Secretary to find out all the paperwork that must be executed every time you offer an employee stock options, when an employee's shares vest, when an employee exercises his/her right, when he/she resigns, and all the possible triggers and scenarios based on your Stock Options Plan.

*****

Key Takeaways:

- Stock options are a great way to attract, motivate and retain talented employees. It's also a good way to conserve cash while attracting talents who are willing to commit to the company long-term to help the company scale.
- Stock options need to be approved by your shareholders and board. Make sure to comply with the approval process and corporate

governance. Check too if there are any local regulations and requirements you need to comply with.
- Equity is very precious so carefully decide on who deserves to be in your stock options plan.
- Once you have a stock options pool, closely keep track of how many have been allocated already to make sure you're still within your approved options' pool.
- Closely work with your Corporate Secretary to ensure that required paperwork is done every time you offer an employee stock options, when an employee's shares vest, when an employee exercises his/her right, when he/she resigns, etc.

8 FUND-RAISING & SHARE-RELATED MATTERS

Raising funds could come in many forms. The more common ways are via loan, shareholder advance, convertible note, SAFE note and equity.

For purposes of discussion, we can focus on convertible notes and equity rounds as these two usually trigger the most questions among new founders. Conversion computations may also apply to SAFE notes as they have similarities with convertible notes. As the name denotes - SAFE which stands for Simple Agreement for Future Equity - SAFE notes are simpler and more straightforward, while convertible notes typically have varying conversion terms.

If you were previously overwhelmed by cap tables, now is also the time to learn to like or even love them. Computing for equity as shown in Chapter 2 Setting up a Company, only requires simple math. Once you understand the logic, everything should be easy. You would be able to easily compute - even on the spot - when talking to prospective investors. Hopefully, by the end of this chapter, you'll fall in love with cap tables.

A Convertible Note as described in Chapter 5 is a form of agreement wherein an investor lends money to a startup, and the investor has an option to convert the debt into shares based on some pre-agreed terms and trigger conditions.

What are the typical components of a Convertible Note?

- **Interest Rate.** Since a convertible note is a form of debt investment, the invested amount earns a rate of interest. The interest in not usually paid in cash, but accrued, which means the value owed to the investor grows over time.
- **Maturity Date.** The maturity date is when the Convertible Note is due and payable to the investor - assuming the note has not yet been converted to equity because there are certain events or conditions that may trigger conversion before the maturity date arrives. Some convertible notes though may have a provision for automatic conversion upon maturity, and for some, the conversion to equity is only an option.
- **Conversion Provisions.** The purpose of a Convertible Note is that it will have an option convert into equity at some point in the future. The most common method of conversion is a qualified financing – or when a subsequent equity investment meets or exceeds a certain threshold. For example, if the qualified financing is set at $10,000,000, this means that if the startup is able to raise an equity investment of at least $10,000,000 in its next round, the Convertible Note converts to equity (even if maturity date has not yet arrived). The amount to be converted to

equity would typically be the original principal plus its accrued interest (unless there is/are other stipulation/s).

- **Conversion Discount.** This is a discount to the price per share of the new equity. For example, if the discount is 20% and the new equity in the qualified financing is sold at $10.00 per share, the convertible note's principal plus accrued interest converts at a share price of $8.00 per share ($10 less 20% discount or $2).
- **Valuation Cap:** This is a hard cap on the conversion price regardless of the price per share on the next round of equity financing. For example, if the valuation cap is set at $20,000,000 but the startup's pre-money valuation in the next round actually reached $30,000,000, this means that the share price to be used as basis for conversion of the investor's principal plus accrued interest would be based on the $20,000,000 pre-money valuation (and not at $30,000,000 pre-money valuation) – assuming the convertible note does not have a discount. If the convertible note has a discount, it has to be determined if applying the valuation cap or the discount would be more favorable to the investor (an example is provided in the succeeding pages).

Some common conversion terms for convertible notes are:
- Pre-money Valuation Cap only (no conversion discount)
- Conversion Discount only (no Valuation Cap)
- Conversion Discount or Pre-Money Valuation, whichever is lower (or more favorable to the Investor)

For illustration purposes to better understand how notes are converted, let's use a simple example where there is a

Conversion Discount and a Valuation Cap. This example will also illustrate how to compute for equity investment since there is a qualified financing trigger condition. Note though that this example uses very basic terms and conditions (in the real setting, there could be a lot of other possible terms, conditions and other variables that can be included in a convertible note).

Convertible Note Terms are as follows:
Principal Amount: $500,000
Interest Rate: 5% p.a.
Maturity Period: 2 years
Terms: 20% discount or $25,000,000 pre-money Valuation Cap, whichever is lower
Qualified Financing: $5,000,000
Type of Shares: Common Shares
Note Holder: JKL Capital

Now, let's say after 10 months, the startup was able to successfully raise equity investments in its Series A round totaling $5,000,000 at a pre-money valuation of $30,000,000. Even if the Convertible Note's maturity is still more than a year away, the conversion of the note is triggered because the qualified financing condition is met.

Let's now determine which is more favorable for the Note Holder, JKL Capital, between the Valuation Cap and Conversion Discount.

Option 1: Convert at a pre-money Valuation Cap of $25,000,000.
Option 2: Convert at a Conversion Discount of 20%
Let's apply the discount:
Pre-money Valuation of the Company is $30,000,000
less 20% discount
=$24,000,000

Between the two options, Option 2 or using the Conversion Discount, yields a lower pre-money amount ($24,000,000 is less than the $25,000,000 pre-money Valuation Cap) which is favorable for JKL Capital, thus, the Conversion Discount will be used as basis for the conversion of JKL's Note.

Let's now compute how much is the current value of JKL's Note which would be converted to equity -
Principal $500,000
Add: Interest $500,000 x (5%/12 months) x 10 months = $20,833.33
Total Amount (Principal + Interest): $520,833.33
The current value of JKL's Note or the total amount to be converted to equity would be $520,833.33.
Note: The computation of interest could also be computed as follows: Annual interest rate divided by 365 days, then multiply by the number of days the note earned interest.

If you want to learn or refresh your mind on how this would impact the company's cap table, let's continue the computations. Let's say below is the latest cap table.

	Outstanding shares	% Equity
Mike	4,500	36%
Joey	3,000	24%
Jane	2,500	20%
ABC Capital	1,250	10%
DEF Capital	750	6%
GHI Capital	500	4%
Total	12,500	100.00%

Let's now compute how many shares, JKL Capital, the Note Holder, would get:

Pre-Money Valuation (discounted) $24,000,000
Divided by Current Outstanding Shares 12,500
= $1,920 price per share

Current Value of JKL's Note $520,833.33.
Divided by $1,920 price per share
= 271.27 shares or rounded down to 271 shares if fractional shares are not allowed

271 shares x $1,920 = $520,320 total payment for shares

$520,833.33 less $520,320
= $513.33 balance to be returned to JKL Capital or it can be booked as a payable by the company to JKL Capital which can be extinguished at a later time (it depends if there are specific terms stipulated in the Convertible Note and/or your accounting policy)

Now, let's compute how many shares will be issued to the Series A investors who are coming in at a $30,000,000 pre-money valuation. Let's assume that all existing shareholders of the company waived their rights to participate in the Series A round and there are 3 investors contributing the following:
MNO Capital - $1,000,000
PQR Capital - $1,500,000
STU Capital - $2,500,000
Total Series A funds raised: $5,000,0000

To compute the share price of the Series A round:
Pre-money valuation $30,000,000
Divided by 12,500 outstanding shares
= $2,400 price per share

Investment amount of MNO Capital $1,000,000
Divided by $2,400 price per share
=416.67 or 417 shares rounded off (or whatever your final terms are)
But assuming that agreement is to round off:
417 shares x $2,400 price per share = $1,000,800 would be MNO's exact investment amount

Investment amount of PQR Capital $1,500,000
Divided by $2,400 price per share
=625 shares
625 shares x $2,400 price per share = $1,500,000 would be PQR's exact investment amount

Investment amount of STU Capital $2,500,000
Divided by $2,400 price per share
=1,041.67 or 1,042 shares rounded off
1,042 shares x $2,400 price per share = $2,500,800 would be STU's exact investment amount

Now let's plug in the shares of all the new investors into the cap table to see the impact of the Series A round on the % ownership of the existing shareholders.

	Seed		Post-Series A (including note conversion but pre-ESOP)	
	Shares	% Equity	Shares	% Equity (pre-ESOP)
Mike	4,500	36.00%	4,500	30.29%
Joey	3,000	24.00%	3,000	20.20%
Jane	2,500	20.00%	2,500	16.83%
ABC Capital	1,250	10.00%	1,250	8.41%
DEF	750	6.00%	750	5.05%

Capital				
GHI Capital	500	4.00%	500	3.37%
JKL Capital			271	1.82%
MNO Capital			417	2.81%
PQR Capital			625	4.21%
STU Capital			1,042	7.01%
Total	12,500	100.00%	14,855	100.00%

Important Reminder: *Due to the limited page width of the book, some columns have been omitted such as historical details of prior rounds and column for Investment Amounts.*
To make a proper cap table, please make sure to:
(1) Reflect the complete names of each shareholder.
(2) Show the detailed history starting from the time of incorporation in the leftmost column to the latest round in the rightmost column.
(3) Each equity event or funding round should have the following columns: Investment Amount ($), # of Shares & % Equity.
(4) Segregate each type of share e.g. common shares, preferred shares.

As you can see in the preceding table in the rightmost column, post-Series A, Mike's ownership goes down to 30.29%. If you remember in Chapter 2, Mike started with a 45% ownership. As a startup keeps on raising funds, the existing shareholders' equity keeps on getting diluted unless they participate in every round pro-rata to their shareholding.

Let's do some quick validations if the cap table computations above are correct.

Series A Pre-money Valuation $30,000,000
Add:
Fair Value of JKL's converted note $650,400 (271 shares x

$2,400 price per share)
MNO's investment $1,000,800
PQR's investment $1,500,000
STU's investment. $2,500,800
Post-money Valuation: $35,652,000

MNO Capital investment $1,000,800
Divided by Post-money Valuation. $35,652,000
= 2.81% equity (it matches MNO's equity in the cap table)

PQR Capital investment $1,500,000
Divided by Post-money Valuation. $35,652,000
= 4.21% equity (it matches PQR's equity in the cap table)

STU Capital investment $2,500,800
Divided by Post-money Valuation $35,652,000
= 7.01% equity (it matches STU's equity in the cap table)

Now let's assume that as part of the Series A term sheet, a 10% Employee Stock Options Plan (ESOP) would be put into place. To compute for it, you need to divide the outstanding shares post-Series A by 90% (100% less 10%) because the outstanding shares should represent 90%, while the ESOP should represent 10%. The number you'll get is the total shares including ESOP, thus, to get the ESOP allocation, you need to deduct the outstanding shares from the total.

Here's the computation for the ESOP allocation:
Outstanding shares post-Series A: 14,855
Divided by 90%
= 16,505.55 or 16,506 (rounded off) would be the total shares including ESOP allocation
16,506 shares less 14,855 outstanding shares = 1,651 shares allocated for ESOP

To validate if ESOP allocation is correct, divide the

number of ESOP allocation by total shares:
1,651 ESOP allocation divided by 16,506 total shares = 10% which was the target allocation of ESOP post-series A round.

Plugging in the ESOP Allocation, below is how the cap table would look like.

	Post-Series A (Pre-ESOP)		**Post Series A, Post-ESOP (fully diluted)**	
	Shares (excluding ESOP)	% Equity	Shares (including ESOP)	% Equity
Mike	4,500	30.29%	4,500	27.26%
Joey	3,000	20.20%	3,000	18.18%
Jane	2,500	16.83%	2,500	15.15%
ABC Capital	1,250	8.41%	1,250	7.57%
DEF Capital	750	5.05%	750	4.54%
GHI Capital	500	3.37%	500	3.03%
JKL Capital	271	1.82%	271	1.64%
MNO Capital	417	2.81%	417	2.53%
PQR Capital	625	4.21%	625	3.79%
STU Capital	1,042	7.01%	1,042	6.31%
ESOP			1,651	10.00%
Total	14,855	100%	16,506	100.00%

The rightmost column in the table above shows the fully

diluted equity post-Series A and post-ESOP where everyone got diluted by 10% because of the 10% ESOP allocation.

Important Reminder:

Due to the limited page width of the book, some columns have been omitted. To make a proper cap table, the cap table should:
(1) Reflect the complete names of each shareholder.
(2) Show the detailed history starting from the time of incorporation in the leftmost column to the latest round in the rightmost column.
(3) Each equity event or funding round should have the following columns: Investment Amount ($), # of Shares & % Equity.
(4) Segregate each type of share e.g. common shares, preferred shares.

This example uses a simplistic scenario where the Note converts to Common Shares and where the subsequent round is also in the form of Common Shares. Since there is only one type of share, all shares can be put together in one column per equity round. However, it's more common to have various types of shares e.g. Common Shares and Preferred Shares. In such case, there should be a different column for Common and Preferred Shares.

Using the same example, let's just say, the shares in JKL's Note and the Series A Round are Preferred Shares. In the succeeding page is how the Post-Series A and Post-ESOP equity (fully diluted) section would look like:

	Outstanding Shares, Post-Seed			Post-Series A, Post-ESOP (fully diluted)				
	Investment	Common Shares	% Equity	Investment	Preferred Shares	ESOP (Common)	Total Shares	% Equity
Mike Smith	$4,500	4,500	36%				4,500	27.26%
Joey Lee	$3,000	3,000	24%				3,000	18.18%
Jane Jones	$2,500	2,500	20%				2,500	15.15%
ABC Capital	$1,000,000	1,250	10%				1,250	7.57%
DEF Capital	$600,000	750	6%				750	4.54%
GHI Capital	$400,000	500	4%				500	3.03%
JKL Capital				$520,320	271		271	1.64%
MNO Capital				$1,000,800	417		417	2.53%
PQR Capital				$1,500,000	625		625	3.79%
STU Capital				$2,500,800	1,042		1,042	6.31%
ESOP						1,651	1,651	10.00%
Total	$2,010,000	12,500	100%	$5,521,920	2,355	1,651	16,506	100.00%

As you may have noticed, the effective % equity is still the same as in the previous scenario wherein all shares were Common Shares. This is because the % of ownership is always based on the number of shares owned. The difference between Common and Preferred shares are rights and features such as voting rights, payment of dividends, claim to earnings, liquidation preference, conversion, among others. Rights and features may vary per share issuance, thus, each of these may entail separate tracking, computations and simulations. They would be best discussed and simulated together with your local expert, lawyer or accountant.

Here's another important piece of advice - when % equity is presented in materials, term sheet and other documents, please make sure you indicate if the equity is fully diluted or not. If it is not fully diluted, you need to put qualifiers e.g. if the indicated equity is pre-conversion of notes, pre-ESOP, etc. so that the investor knows that the % equity would still be further diluted. For example, if it's indicated that the % equity is pre-conversion of notes, then the investor knows that equity would be further diluted once existing notes are converted. Or if it's indicated that the % equity is pre-ESOP, then the investor knows that equity would be further diluted once ESOP is put into place. To avoid any misinterpretation on how the fully diluted equity shall be computed, the best way is to put a simulated cap table in the annex of your Investment Agreement. Since it's just a simulated cap table, please make sure to indicate all variable assumptions in the document (e.g. for a conversion of note, what were your assumptions for pre-money valuation, the period for the computation of interest rate, etc.) so that in case those exact assumptions do not materialize, the investor knows that the final fully diluted equity may differ from the simulated cap table shown in the annex of your Investment Agreement.

Finally, when funding gets credited to your company's bank account, it is definitely going to be a joyous moment - no more sleepless nights worrying about where to get money to fund your operations. You can finally focus on growing the business without worrying about funds – at least for the next 12 to 24 months. But sometimes, out of excitement, founders forget to inform their accountants about the details of the funding. It is not enough for your accountant to know the amount, he/she also needs to know if the funds will be booked as a loan, cash advance, deposit for future subscription, or equity. You also need to furnish him/her with a copy of the signed agreement/s so he/she can properly book the entries and capture the details.

As a guide, here's a quick checklist when you are fund-raising:

Sample Checklist when fund-raising

- Whatever type of instrument or fund-raising you plan to do, please check with your Corporate Secretary on what needs to be circulated to shareholders and/or board e.g., notices and waivers and the prescribed period, before you can officially start talking to prospective investors outside of existing shareholders. This is to make sure you do not violate any shareholder rights as some existing shareholders may want to exercise their pro-rata rights.
- When you discuss your fund-raising terms with prospective investors, always disclose if there are any stock options' allocation, existing convertible notes and/or other stock warrants so that prospective investors know that the % equity based on post-money valuation is not a fully-diluted % ownership. And when you do your cap

tables, always have a column that shows the fully diluted % equity. To avoid any misinterpretation, have a simulated cap table to show the fully diluted equity as part of the annex of your Investment Agreement.

- Build your own cap table instead of using online templates because the terms and conditions may greatly vary from deal to deal, from round to round, and even from investor to investor, and online templates may not be able to capture the nuances of some terms and conditions. In your cap table, show the detailed history starting from the time of incorporation in the leftmost column to the latest shareholding in the rightmost column. Properly label columns for each round and if some are only simulations (e.g. conversion), indicate in the column heading. Also, make sure you have a column for fully-diluted % equity if there are existing equity-related obligations to see the ultimate impact on the shareholding. Make your cap tables as detailed as you can – including notes and computations – because as you have more financing rounds, or simply just over time, you may start forgetting some details per round. Notes and detailed computations would help you refresh your memory at how you arrived at the figures.

- If you are using a different lawyer to draft your investment agreements, please make sure to also coordinate closely with your Corporate Secretary in finalizing investment agreements. Make sure your Corporate Secretary knows everything as he/she should prepare all the supporting documents e.g., minutes of the meeting and board resolutions which are part of the corporate compliance requirements when you are fundraising, and also so that he/she can guide you on

what you need to secure from incoming shareholders as part of the Know-Your-Customer (KYC) requirements.
- Once you get the fully signed copies of the Investment Agreements, please furnish your Corporate Secretary with a complete set for his/her file.
- Inform your accountant about the details of your fund-raising activity including how to properly book the amounts e.g., if it is a loan, cash advance, equity. Furnish him/her with copies of the documents so he/she can properly book the correct entries e.g. if there is premium payment or additional paid in capital (APIC). Also, please instruct your accountant to pay any taxes due. He/she would only know the taxes due if you furnish him/her with the proper documents. Usually, there are deadlines on tax payments depending on the date of the transaction, so please make sure that you inform your accountant about the transactions on time, so you won't incur any penalties.
- Depending on your domicile, when you are expecting a huge amount from an investor, you might have to inform your bank in advance and submit some supporting documents to your bank in compliance with local anti-money laundering regulations.
- When you get the funds from the investors, please do not forget to update your Corporate Secretary as he/she may need to file some paperwork with government bureaus and also issue share certificates (if it is an equity raise).
- Double-check if there are any other post-closing requirements stated in your definitive agreements. Make sure you deliver all the commitments stated there to your investors within the time frame

agreed upon as there may be serious repercussions and consequences if you fail to do so.
- [ ] Consult with a local expert if there are any other requirements you need to comply with.

In case you have convertible notes that are due for conversion, here's also a checklist which you can use as a guide:

Sample Checklist when Converting Notes

- [ ] Update your cap table.
- [ ] Please check with your Corporate Secretary on what needs to be circulated and signed by existing shareholders and/or board in relation to the conversion of the Note, as well as any Know-Your-Customer (KYC) requirements needed from the incoming shareholders.
- [ ] If you are using a different lawyer to draft the conversion agreements, please make sure to also have them reviewed by your Corporate Secretary to ensure that the agreements are in alignment with existing agreements.
- [ ] Once you get the fully signed copies of the Investment Agreements, please furnish your Corporate Secretary with a complete set for his/her file. He/she may also need to file some paperwork with government bureaus and also issue the share certificates.
- [ ] Inform your accountant about the details of the conversion so he/she can properly book the transaction/s, as well as make adjustments in the balance sheet. Furnish him/her with copies of the documents so he/she can properly book the correct entries e.g. if there is premium payment or additional paid in capital (APIC). Also, please instruct your accountant to pay any taxes due.

He/she would only know the taxes due after you furnish him/her with the proper documents. Usually, there are deadlines on tax payments depending on the date of the transaction so please make sure that you inform your accountant about the transactions on time so you won't incur any penalties.
- Consult with a local expert if there are any other requirements you need to comply with.

At some point, you might also have some secondary sale of shares – meaning existing shareholders selling their shares to others. Though this is a transaction between the existing shareholder and the buyer (and does not have any impact on the company's capital as the startup does not get any share in the sale proceeds), there are still corporate compliance requirements that need to be executed as existing shareholders have pro-rata rights.

Here is a checklist which you can use as a guide:

Sample Checklist for Secondary Sale of Shares

- Check with your Corporate Secretary on the process for secondary sale and what needs to be circulated and signed by shareholders and/or board in relation to a secondary sale (e.g., notices, waivers, etc. as existing shareholders typically have the right to buy shares pro-rata to their shareholding before the shares can be offered to external parties) within a prescribed period.
- Check with your Corporate Secretary on what are the other requirements needed for the secondary sale transaction e.g. retrieval of original share certificate of the seller as the Corporate Secretary needs to cancel it, Know-Your-Customer (KYC) requirements from the buyer of shares, etc.

- ☐ Request for fully signed copies of the Stock Purchase Agreements from the seller and furnish your Corporate Secretary with copies for his/her file. He/she may also need to file some paperwork with government bureaus, as well as issue a new share certificate. Also, check if there are any tax payments to be made and if you need to secure tax payment proofs from the seller and the buyer.
- ☐ Inform your accountant about the details of the transaction. There won't be any impact on the company's capital but at least he/she can take note of the change in shareholder/s. Also check if there are any tax payments to be made and if he/she needs copies of payment proofs from the seller and the buyer.
- ☐ Update your cap table file to reflect the name/s of the new shareholders.
- ☐ Consult with a local expert if there are any other requirements you need to comply with.

One final advice - once you have investors, make sure to deliver your commitments to them. If you foresee any delay in delivering them, it is better to proactively inform them than wait for them to follow you up. Also, give them regular updates and share with them both the good news and the bad news as they might be able to help you with your challenges.

Below is a simple template which you can use during your early days. It is just short and very easy to prepare but contains the most important things your investors and advisors should know. But later on, when you have more resources and bandwidth, you can include more details in your reports such as detailed KPI tracking, latest P&L, balance sheet and cashflow forecast.

Sample Investor Email Update Template

Description of your Startup: Put a one sentence pitch to refresh everyone on what your startup is about.

Snapshot of your Core Metrics:
List down 3 to 5 of the most important metrics you track to give your investors a brief summary of how your business is doing.
Examples:
- Monthly sales revenues
- Growth metrics e.g. signups, paying customers
- Conversion rates
- Tech or R&D Progress

Snapshot of Financial Metrics:
- Cash in bank
- Monthly burn
- Cash runway

Key Highlights:
List your top 3 highlights or key achievements.

Challenges:
List your top 3 challenges so your investors and advisors would be aware of them and who knows, some of them might be able to help or offer advice.

Top priorities for the next month:
State 3 to 5 goals you are targeting for next month.

Where you need help:
State 1 to 3 areas where you think your investors and advisors could help you with e.g. introduction to potential clients, referral to potential hires.

You can send this report to your investors and advisors every month via email. This way, your investors and advisors are aware of your startup's overall health, and should there be challenges, they could be a part of your journey and help you. Always remember - if your investors can help you, they would - as it is in their best interest if your company succeeds.

*****

Key Takeaways:

- The work does not stop after closing a financing round and securing the money. Be mindful of all the obligations that need to be fulfilled e.g. filing all the required paperwork, paying taxes, issuing share certificates, delivering post-closing commitments to investors, etc.
- Make sure to inform your corporate secretary and closely work with him/her from end-to-end of the process as he/she will be in charge in facilitating most of the corporate compliance requirements. He/she would not know the details and know at what stage you are in the process unless the two of you regularly align.
- Make sure to also inform your accountant so he/she can properly book the amounts and reflect them in your balance sheet. And even when advances or notes are converted to equity, you still need to inform your accountant so he/she can make the adjustments accordingly in the company's balance sheet.
- Deliver what you promised to your investors so they would likely participate again in your future fund-raising rounds. You would want your existing shareholders to participate in your succeeding rounds as this would show strong

shareholder confidence which is a good sign to attract new investors.

CONCLUSION

The moment you launch your startup, it's going to be an endless string of new goals, product roll-outs, priorities and responsibilities.

Improving your products and/or services, gaining traction and generating revenues would tend to occupy your day-to-day grind, so much so that all other things become secondary. Except that when these secondary things (no matter how small) accumulate over time, they can create serious problems for your company - whether discrepancies in your financial statements, statutory violations and penalties, or worse, loss in trust by investors and filed lawsuits. You would be lucky if they could be fixed, but there are also cases that cannot be fixed or wherein the solution comes at a very high cost. What you have worked so hard for several years could easily be wiped out by one careless oversight. Why take the risk if you can actually do something to prevent some of these from happening?

As discussed in every chapter of the book, by establishing frameworks and ensuring that processes are in place right from the start, you can prevent avoidable mistakes, errors and oversights from happening.

Here's a quick recap:

- When starting discussions with potential co-founders, you have to mutually agree and be clear with the expectations and deliverables from each one, and also agree on the terms in such case as when one is unable to deliver his/her end of the bargain – because no matter how giddy you are about the company vision during the planning stage, ugly things can happen. Along the way, some co-founders may not give the same level of effort, spend as much time as other co-founders, are unable to deliver what was promised, abandon the project for another opportunity, or sometimes undergo a personal crisis which prevents them from performing their duties. Such situations have happened even among family members, best friends and couples, and it could also happen to you. So make sure everything you agreed upon is on paper.

- Thoroughly think about your corporate structure, check if there is any required sequence in setting up multiple entities (e.g. holding company, operating entity), carefully plan the timing of your incorporation and familiarize yourself with local regulations and requirements. If scoped and done properly, you won't get into trouble for any violations in areas such as foreign ownership restrictions, required license/s to operate, operating outside of your primary purpose and other local regulations. Plus, you won't waste time and money in incorporating entities that may have to be dissolved at very high costs.

- Design your Accounting & Finance processes well so you will have accurate financials. Whatever you are presenting to your management and board should match the financial statements being filed by your accountant. With accurate financials, you know the true state of your company – not just how are you doing versus budget, but if you are losing or making money and if you are becoming operationally cost-efficient as you scale. You will also be able to precisely predict your cash runway and won't be caught off-guard that the funds that you thought would last for a year are about to be depleted on the sixth month. Getting your financials right and clean would also protect your company from possible tax exposure and non-compliance and save you from potentially huge tax penalties (other than the high costs, these won't make you look good either to prospective investors during the due diligence process). Allowing your company to have messy and inaccurate financials is a sure way to self-sabotage your startup's chance of success.

- Employer-employee relationships always start on a happy note, but there will be times when things could get sour. To protect yourself, from the very beginning, make sure you are compliant with local labor laws such as what are the required number of working hours, who is qualified for overtime pay and how is it computed, statutory benefits, etc. The wording of your employment contracts and correspondences to employees should also be precise as those can also be used as potential sources for loopholes or misinterpretations. Carefully educate yourself on the labor code of your domicile especially when it comes to treating and firing employees because other than reputational risks, labor suits could be really expensive. Also, make sure to have an updated and comprehensive checklist in place for terminated and/or resigning employees to protect the company's confidential information and files from unauthorized access and use.

- Even if you have a lawyer or pool of lawyers, make it your accountability to understand all kinds of contracts and agreements that you enter into. At the end of the day, you cannot blame anyone for ending up with a bad deal once you've put your signature in a document. Signing it means you have read it and you agree to all the terms in the contract. And though corporate compliance requires a lot of tedious paperwork and administrative work, you have to diligently do it. You do not have to necessarily do it on your own, but you need to drive it as you are the one who knows all the important transactions of the company that need board or shareholder approval. Your Corporate Secretary would have to depend on you to inform him/her. An oversight in legal and/or corporate governance can have serious legal and financial repercussions, and it also reflects a lot about how you value your commitments to your shareholders, board and other stakeholders.

- As you grow your business, your files would accumulate. But every now and then, you need to refer to old transactions to check past terms and conditions. Unfortunately, digging up files in old email threads or chat messages (if you can even remember where they could be found in the first place) could be very time-consuming. Asking your team members to help you trace email threads or files is not productive either as it is time taken away from doing the real work. Thus, setting up a Master Data Room which would serve as a centralized repository of all your company's important files is a powerful tool you can have. Easily pull out the required info any time you need it and without the need to bother other team members. And once you have a Master Data Room, you can easily set up customized Investor Data Rooms for prospective investors and/or existing shareholders as you can easily duplicate folders or copy files from the Master Data Room.

- Employee Stock Options are meant to attract talent and incentivize and retain valuable key team members. Since this has an impact on the cap table, make sure to secure approval from your shareholders and board before implementing one. Plus, make sure to check what are the local regulations and requirements surrounding it since there are domiciles where filing in a government bureau is required. Once approved, abide by what you, your shareholders and Board have agreed upon in relation to the awarding of shares, the recipients and the terms and conditions. You also need to have a tracker to make sure you know how many shares have been allocated to employees already, so that at any time, you know what the remaining available shares are for future talents you want to attract, motivate, reward and retain.

- Fund-Raising & Share-Related Matters is one thing that a founder has to know by heart. Properly building your cap table and putting in as much as details as you can per financing round would help you recall all the details at how you arrived at computations and easily address questions when confronted by prospective investors.

As a cardinal rule, any proposal or plan that may impact your company's equity has to be taken up with your existing shareholders and board, so please make sure to closely coordinate with your Corporate Secretary so he/she can assist you in complying with all the obligations stated in your articles, by-laws and shareholders' agreement. Also, when signing investment agreements, there are certain terms and conditions in there which you promised to deliver to your investors – make sure you deliver them on time. The last thing you want to happen is to end up being negligent, or worse, be accused of breach of contract where damages could cost not just the company but may cost you as well.

Invest time and effort in implementing frameworks, designing your processes, and regularly aligning with your team and/or service providers. The rewards you will reap from them would be valuable in the long-term. You will also be able to focus better on growing your business as you don't have to worry about little things falling through the cracks which could lead to operational inefficiencies, integrity and reputational risks, tax penalties, labor complaints and lawsuits.

Though the checklists presented in the book are not exhaustive and they are not customized to a particular domicile, you can use them as a starting point to build your own customized checklists for your startup. Talk to local expert/s and get their opinion on what should be edited, added and/or if there is any required sequence to the process or series of events/transactions. As you do a wider variety of transactions and as local regulations change, you will also discover more items to add to your checklists so make it a habit to regularly update your checklists.

Some final words of advice:

- Protect and preserve your equity as much as you can and be mindful of equity dilution. The more frequent and the more funds you raise, the smaller your equity becomes. Thus, make sure whatever funds you raise, you spend wisely and purposefully for the growth and success of the company.

- Even when your lawyer or accountant say it's alright to sign an agreement or sign financial statements, review everything before signing. You have to take it upon yourself to understand everything. If you see something that you do not understand, ask. There is no such thing as a stupid question. Not asking clarifying questions when you do not understand something is what is stupid. It is always in your best interest to fully understand everything in a document because the last thing that you want to happen is regretting entering into something that got you or your company into trouble. It is in being curious and asking the right questions that would make you sharper.

- Learn how to ask the right questions because there are times when essential information is inadvertently omitted, or potential scenarios are not considered or foreseen, because the right questions were never asked. You cannot solely rely on your accountant, lawyer, employee or service provider to think about all of these. Critical points could surface during the review process and be considered - but only if you ask the right questions. To challenge the experts who are helping you, you can start with blanket questions like: This is something new to me. Is there anything else I should know about a transaction like this? Is there anything else I should be wary of? Is there anything that needs to be paid, filed or complied with for this kind of transaction? Are there other potential scenarios not covered or identified in the agreement? Are there enough provisions and clauses in the agreement to protect the company, its officers and me? As an exercise, you can think of potential scenarios and see if there is something in place in the agreement that covers each one and that sufficiently protects your company, the officers and you.

- Your accountant, corporate secretary or HR person would not know all your company's transactions unless you inform them or share with them copies of relevant agreements. Do not expect them to know, follow through or do the compliance part if they do not know the details of a certain transaction in the first place. Make sure to copy them in emails or regularly align with them so nothing is left unaccounted for or forgotten. When these small, forgotten things accumulate, they could be a big problem, or worse, a single oversight could cost you your entire company.

- No matter how busy you are, review your finances. Even if you highly trust the people who handle your finance and accounting, there is no better and more honest financial steward than you. Fraudulent transactions within a company are usually left undetected until the last minute because they are committed by people whom owners trust.

- Creating checklists (which is the common tool suggested throughout the book) may require a bit of work the first time you'll make one, but as you build and update your checklists, their usefulness would be many times over. Invest some time and effort to create them as they would help you organize your startup smarter and better. If you accept that it's only human to have oversights, that says a lot about you. There are things that can be anticipated and pre-planned and there are tools available to minimize oversights, lapses and inefficiencies and it is in your power to prevent these avoidable mistakes.

Startup life is not easy, but the journey would be a little smoother and less painful if you set things right from the start.

The Organized Startup

ANNEX

Sample Cap Table

	Incorporation			Seed Round				Post-Series A, Post-ESOP (fully diluted)				
	Investment	Shares (Common)	% Equity	Investment	Shares (Common)	Total Shares	% Equity	Investment	Preferred Shares	ESOP (Common)	Total Shares	% Equity
Mike Smith	$4,500	4,500	45%			4,500	36%				4,500	27.26%
Joey Lee	$3,000	3,000	30%			3,000	24%				3,000	18.18%
Jane Jones	$2,500	2,500	25%			2,500	20%				2,500	15.15%
ABC				$1,000,000	1,250	1,250	10%				1,250	7.57%
DEF				$600,000	750	750	6%				750	4.54%
GHI				$400,000	500	500	4%				500	3.03%
JKL								$520,320	271		271	1.64%
MNO								$1,000,800	417		417	2.53%
PQR								$1,500,000	625		625	3.79%
STU								$2,500,800	1,042		1,042	6.31%
ESOP										1,651	1,651	10.00%
Total	$10,000	10,000	100%	$2,000,000	2,500	12,500	100%	$5,521,920	2,355	1,651	16,506	100%

Note: Please make sure to reflect the complete names of investors in your cap table. Due to the limited space, only acronyms were used in the sample table.

To make a proper cap table, the cap table should:
(1) Reflect the complete names of each shareholder. Due to the limited page width of the book, complete names of investors have not been reflected in the sample cap table.
(2) Show the detailed history starting from the time of incorporation in the leftmost column to the latest round in the rightmost column.
(3) Each equity event or funding round should have the following columns: Investment Amount ($), # of Shares & % Equity.
(4) Segregate each type of share e.g. common shares, preferred shares.

Sample Checklist in Organizing Accounting & Finance

- [ ] Make a checklist of tax filing deadlines throughout the year
- [ ] Understand all applicable taxes for your company's type of transactions
- [ ] Map out potential tax exposure for your kind of business so you can prevent them from happening
- [ ] Have templates for your invoice, official receipt, delivery receipt, etc.
- [ ] Open bank account/s - ideally, one bank account for collections and one bank account for disbursements
- [ ] Decide on what accounting software to use
- [ ] Brief your accountant on the following:
    - Revenue recognition
    - Classification of revenue streams
    - Accrual policy
    - Classification of Cost of Sales (COS)
    - Classification of overhead expenses
    - What expenses need to be capitalized
    - Depreciation policy of assets
- [ ] Accounting processes (approval process for request for payments, lead time for processing payments, disbursement schedules, etc.)
- [ ] Regular reports you want to see (Income statement, Cashflow Statement, Balance Sheet, etc.), your preferred report formats, the frequency of reports and who are the authorized recipients of the reports
- [ ] Corporate credit card guidelines
- [ ] Collection process
- [ ] Scope other items that need to be added to the list depending on what is applicable to your domicile and the nature of your business

Sample Checklist in Organizing HR

- ☐ Know all employer-related obligations and familiarize yourself with the local labor laws
- ☐ Determine what are the required minimum employee benefits and statutory benefits
- ☐ Understand the differences of the various types of engagement e.g., full-time employee versus a contractual employee versus a consultant, and make sure that your contracts reflect the proper wording/terms for each
- ☐ Have ready templates for job offers, employment contracts, consultancy contracts, etc.
- ☐ Have your pre-employment checklist – what are the things you would require new hires to submit
- ☐ Design your employee onboarding process
- ☐ Coordinate with Accounting in setting up the payroll account and discuss the following:
  - Payroll process
  - Cut-off dates
  - Payroll Computations
  - Attendance reports
  - Policy on leaves and leaves' tracking
- ☐ Process for resigning employees
- ☐ Have a system in place for properly organizing employee files
- ☐ Performance feedback and appraisal process
- ☐ Exit process for resigning employees
- ☐ Scope other items that need to be added to the list depending on what is applicable to your domicile and the nature of your business

Sample Turnover Checklist for a Resigning Accountant

- [ ] Retrieval of tax filing returns
- [ ] Retrieval of the online tax filing access (please also make sure to update the authorized person/s and/or email addresses associated with your company and registered in your tax bureau)
- [ ] List of the contact details of suppliers, vendors, partners, service providers (e.g. auditor, tax agent) and clients he/she regularly corresponds with
- [ ] Schedule of recurring transactions
- [ ] Templates, booklets or pads of the Company's Invoice, Statements of Account, Official Receipt, Delivery Receipt, etc.
- [ ] Original proofs of payment for statutory benefits
- [ ] Past years' Audited Financial Statements (AFS)
- [ ] Other Accounting Files
- [ ] Online Banking Access - please make sure you remove your accountant's access
- [ ] Retrieve bank passbooks and checkbooks
- [ ] Process on how to remove your accountant as an authorized person in your corporate bank account/s and how to assign a new authorized person
- [ ] Disable your resigning accountant's access to your accounting software. If you plan to use a different software moving forward, ask the resigning accountant to extract soft copies of all accounting files and financial statements
- [ ] Scope other items that need to be added to the list depending on what is applicable to your domicile and the nature of your business

Sample Turnover Checklist for a Resigning Employee

- [ ] Retrieve all company files and documents
- [ ] Turnover of all pending items and supporting files and/or latest email threads on these items (and endorsement to the people he/she is corresponding with)
- [ ] List of the person's external office contacts and their contact details
- [ ] Retrieve all company-owned equipment and assets that were assigned to the person e.g. laptop, ID, HMO card, etc.
- [ ] Make sure to inform third-party vendors to terminate the resigning employee's subscription to employee benefits e.g. HMO plan
- [ ] Deactivate the employee's email address
- [ ] Deactivate the employee's door access code
- [ ] Disable and deactivate the access of the person in all systems, apps, accounts and websites such as:
    - company's social media accounts
    - shared folders and drives
    - company domains/websites
    - other third party apps
- [ ] If files of the resigning employee are in a shared drive, make arrangement for the transfer of ownership of the files before terminating his/her account
- [ ] Remove the person from all official chat groups and channels
- [ ] Update the company website if there is a page for management team and the resigning employee is featured there
- [ ] Update the company's list of signatories if the resigning employee is an authorized signatory
- [ ] Scope other items applicable to the nature of your business and local setting

Sample Turnover Checklist for an Outgoing Corporate Secretary

Retrieve the following:
- ☐ Signed Minutes
- ☐ Signed Board or Directors' Resolutions
- ☐ Signed Secretary's Certificates
- ☐ Signed Waivers
- ☐ Signed Subscription Agreements
- ☐ Signed Shareholders' Agreement
- ☐ Signed Deeds of Adherence to the Shareholders' Agreement
- ☐ Signed Stock Purchase Agreements
- ☐ Stock Transfer Book
- ☐ Any other share-related documents
- ☐ Share Certificates
- ☐ Company Seal
- ☐ Receiving copies of filed documents in government bureaus
- ☐ Other Corporate documents safe-kept by the Corporate Secretary

Sample Checklist where Board Approval is Required (just remove/add applicable items)

- Amendment/s to the Articles of Incorporation or By-laws
- Entering into any agreements that could be of material importance (e.g. license contracts, customer contracts, vendor contracts, consulting agreements, lease agreements, etc.)
- Issuance of dividends
- Borrowing or lending money
- Annual budget
- Hiring and/or terminating senior management (or amending terms of their employment)
- Adopting new employee benefit plans
- Sale or other distribution of company assets
- Anything that is equity-related (e.g. issuance of new shares, transfer of shares, increase in authorized capital stock, creation of a new type of shares)
- Entering into a contract with a related party
- Election of officers
- Assignment or updating of authorized signatories
- Appointment of the company's auditor
- Opening of a bank account
- Investment in a company
- Dissolution or winding up of the company
- Scope other items specified in your articles, by-laws, shareholders' agreement, and other corporate documents, and take note of all the prescribed period required per type of transaction

Sample Folder Structure for a Company's Master Data Room

- ☐ Audited Financial Statements
- ☐ Capitalization Table
- ☐ Client Contracts
- ☐ Convertible Notes
- ☐ Corporate Documents
- ☐ Employee Stock Options (ESOP)
- ☐ Financials
- ☐ HR
- ☐ Intellectual Property Documents
- ☐ Lease Contracts
- ☐ Marketing Materials
- ☐ Market Research
- ☐ Memorandum of Agreements (MOAs)
- ☐ Minutes and Resolutions
- ☐ Non-Disclosure Agreements
- ☐ Promissory Notes
- ☐ Shareholders' Agreement
- ☐ Subscription Agreements /Investment Agreements
- ☐ Share Certificates & Receiving Copies of Share Certificates
- ☐ Stock Purchase Agreements / Share Transfer Documents
- ☐ Technology
- ☐ Term Sheets
- ☐ Vendor Contracts
- ☐ Voting Agreements
- ☐ Add any other folder applicable to your business

Sample Folder Structure for an Investor Data Room

- Audited Financial Statements
- Capitalization Table
- Convertible Notes
- Corporate Documents
- Employee Stock Options (ESOP)
- Financials
- HR
- Intellectual Property Documents
- Marketing Materials
- Market Research
- Minutes and Resolutions
- Promissory Notes
- Shareholders' Agreement
- Subscription Agreements /Investment Agreements
- Stock Purchase Agreements / Share Transfer Documents
- Technology
- Voting Agreements

Sample Compliance Checklist when you are Fund-raising

- Inform your Corporate Secretary so he/she can prepare what needs to be circulated to shareholders and/or board e.g., notices and waivers within the prescribed period, before you can officially start talking to prospective investors outside of existing shareholders
- If you are using a different lawyer to draft your investment agreements, please make sure to also coordinate closely with your Corporate Secretary since your Corporate Secretary needs to prepare all the supporting documents related to the fund-raise e.g., minutes of the meeting and directors' resolutions
- Once you get the fully signed copies of the Investment Agreements, please furnish your Corporate Secretary with a complete set for his/her file
- Inform your accountant about the details of the fund-raise including how to properly book the amounts. Furnish him/her with copies of the documents and instruct him/her to pay any taxes due
- Update the cap table
- Double-check if there are any other post-closing requirements stated in your definitive agreements and make sure to deliver them within the prescribed period
- Issue stock certificate (if an equity round)
- Consult with your Corporate Secretary if there are any other requirements you need to comply with

Sample Investor Email Update Template

Description of your Startup: Put a one sentence pitch to refresh everyone on what your startup is about.

Snapshot of your Core Metrics:
List down 3 to 5 of the most important metrics you track to give your investors a brief summary of how your business is doing.
Examples:
- Monthly sales revenues
- Growth metrics e.g. signups, paying customers
- Conversion rates
- Tech or R&D Progress

Snapshot of Financial Metrics:
- Cash in bank
- Monthly burn
- Cash runway

Key Highlights:
List your top 3 highlights or key achievements.

Challenges:
List your top 3 challenges so your investors and advisors would be aware of them and who knows, some of them might be able to help or offer advice.

Top priorities for the next month:
State 3 to 5 goals you are targeting for next month.

Where you need help:
State 1 to 3 areas where you think your investors and advisors could help you with e.g. introduction to potential clients, referral to potential hires.

MESSAGE FROM THE AUTHOR

Thank you for reading The Organized Startup. I hope the lessons would help you in your startup journey.

If you enjoyed the book, kindly leave feedback on Amazon.com so others may discover it too. This book is self-published so the only way people would discover it is through readers like you.

Please also get copies or recommend the book to your founder friends and management team. The Organized Startup is available in kindle, paperback and hardcover via Amazon.

To send me a message, you may email me at mao.emica@gmail.com.

Wishing you success!

Emica Mao

www.ingramcontent.com/pod-product-compliance
Lightning Source LLC
Chambersburg PA
CBHW071509220526
45472CB00003B/961